London

Where to quaff WINE in the capital

Another fun wine product from

Published by
Chonkychonks Ltd
60 East St Helen Street
Abingdon
Oxon. OX14 5EB

Tel.: 01235 535 685
Fax: 01235 537 312
Email: editor@quaffers.co.uk
Web: **www.quaffers.co.uk**

ISBN 0-9541104-0-4

Designed and typeset by Mary Thurston & studio@d-blue.com

Printed by The Alden Press, Oxford

Distributed by Portfolio Books Ltd, London

Are you a wine quaffer?

I hope so, because this book is for you.

I started ChonkyChonks in 1999 to make education about wine more fun, less stuffy, but still useful. Quaffing wine is something many of us already enjoy with gusto, but as your knowledge and passion grows, so does the pleasure.

Quaffers® London is our first book (but not the last), and joins a small selection of other products that we have created. We have packed this guide full of places where you can enjoy wines by the glass or by the bottle, from cheap and cheerful to ultra-sophisticated. There's something in here for every personality, every palate, and every pocket. Believe me, there are some gems.

In the past decade there has been a major revolution in drinking habits. Gone are the days when quaffers were happy to risk a glass from the dusty bottle of already-opened red with a cork bunged in the top, or a non-descript medium or dry white from the cooler box on the wall. We have all developed quite a taste for the grape, and there is no shortage of establishments rushing to provide quality and choice where only a few years ago there was none.

We have visited all of the venues listed, and many, many more besides. We don't believe in reviewing places just to tell you how bad they might be, so every listing in this guide is one which we would be happy to return to. London has such a variety of places to quaff wine that if one bar doesn't suit you, there is sure to be another to fit the bill.

Look out too for some additional features that we have included, such as how to tell if your wine is in good condition, less familiar grapes to try, or just how to decode some of the language on a wine list or label. Don't miss the Wine Walks either – a chance to see the sights and quench your thirst on the way.

But I shouldn't take credit for this book because I didn't write it: Mary, our editor, did. I am delighted with the result and thank Mary for all her hard work and considerable talent, which ensured that the project came to fruition.

I hope you have fun quaffing in the capital. Let us know!

Heather

Heather Miller
heather@chonkychonks.co.uk

Acknowledgements

Editorial Staff

Editor: Mary Thurston
Deputy Editor: Heather Miller
Art Editor: Andrew Jones/studio@d-blue.com
Photographs: Mary Thurston
Editorial Team: Catherine Dale, Emily Exton, Ashley Hicks, Stuart Miller, Anna Russell

Thanks

Victoria Alers-Hankey, Gill Barnes, Cornwall Wine Tasting Group, John Downie, Gisela Gledhill, Andrew Jones, Dave Jones, Paul Kendall, Ruth McNulty, Anne-Marie Plumer, Johanna and Maurice Pope, Doug Thurston, Mick Tomlinson, John Watson

Contents

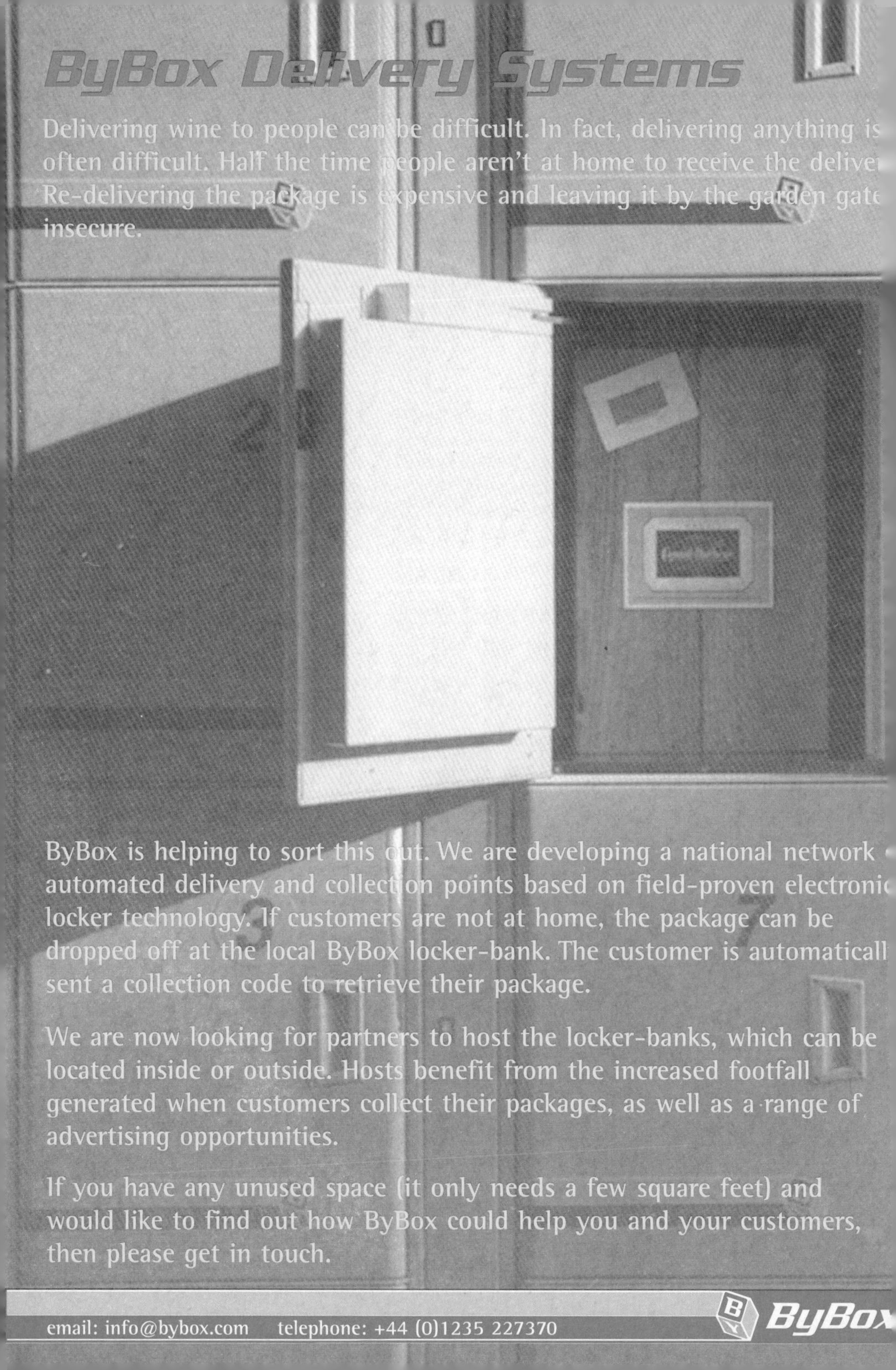
ByBox Delivery Systems
Delivering wine to people can be difficult. In fact, delivering anything i
often difficult. Half the time people aren't at home to receive the delive
Re-delivering the package is expensive and leaving it by the garden gat
insecure.
ByBox is helping to sort this out. We are developing a national network
automated delivery and collection points based on field-proven electroni
locker technology. If customers are not at home, the package can be
dropped off at the local ByBox locker-bank. The customer is automaticall
sent a collection code to retrieve their package.
We are now looking for partners to host the locker-banks, which can be
located inside or outside. Hosts benefit from the increased footfall
generated when customers collect their packages, as well as a range of
advertising opportunities.
If you have any unused space (it only needs a few square feet) and
would like to find out how ByBox could help you and your customers,
then please get in touch.
email: info@bybox.com telephone: +44 (0)1235 227370
ByBox

Quaffers® London is best used with a comprehensive street guide in order to locate both transport connections and street addresses. Where it's difficult to find a venue, the reviews will help you with directions.

- Listings are grouped according to the nearest London Underground (Tube) stop, or occasionally a railway station. These are listed alphabetically, but Quaffers® London includes only those stations with listed venues nearby
- Where a venue is more or less equidistant from another transport connection, this is indicated by a Tube or railway logo after the venue's name.

Use the key below to interpret the basic information in each listing:

- Decide in which area you are likely to be enjoying wine, find the nearest transport, look up that section of the book, and take your pick
- If you know the bar's name already, or prefer to make a selection based on criteria other than the nearest station, use the Index at the back of the book or see the Contents page to help
- Bar chains are a reality of London life. The main chains are listed in a separate section with a brief review of what is offered. If you come across a bar in a mini-chain, and it has not been listed, use the alphabetical venue index to find a review for its sister-bar. In most cases the name will not have been used by another venue
- While most venues do not require bookings, we recommend that you phone in advance if timing or seating are important. Many of the venues are available to hire for private parties – just ask!
- Beware that the majority of bars in the City of London (the business district) are only open Monday to Friday, and tend to close sooner than many pubs in the early part of the week. Some venues close before time if business is quiet – be prepared to be flexible
- Opening hours are dictated by the kind of licence held by a venue. Even if a venue is shown as opening earlier for breakfast or coffee, alcohol is not served before 11am. Check with the venue if you are unsure
- Refer to the extra sections following this page for further information about choosing wines, how to know if the wine you buy is in good condition, how to taste wine, looking out for more unusual grape varieties, and Wine Walks through the capital.

Please tell us if you know of a top quaffing spot anywhere in London, especially in different transport areas, so we can share the good news in our next edition! Use the Freepost Business Reply Card at the back of the book and be entered into our monthly prize draw.

Understanding the jargon

Have you ever looked at a wine list or label and been overwhelmed by the language of it? Has this forced you to fall back on a familiar grape or region when you really wanted to experiment and try something new?

Sometimes the jargon can be a real barrier to getting the most from the world of wine. Quaffers® aims to demystify some of the terminology so you can be more confident about choosing wine, particularly if you are doing so on behalf of others. The days of apologising to your host for the bottle you are about to hand over, or of playing 'Pass the Parcel' with the wine list in bars or restaurants can be behind you!

If you can't find the term you need on this list, make a note and Ask the Expert at **www.quaffers.co.uk** when you get home from quaffing.

Sparkling Wines

Blanc de blancs	Sparkling wine made exclusively from white grapes
Blanc de noirs	Sparkling wine made exclusively from black grapes
Brut	Bone dry
Cava	Spanish sparkling wine made by the traditional method
Champagne	Must come from the French region of the same name to carry this on the label
Cuvée	Blend, particularly of sparkling wines, but also applied to still wines
Demi-Sec	Medium-dry
Méthode Traditionnelle	Sparkling wine made in the same way as Champagne
Prosecco	Italian sparkling wine, light and dry
Sec	Dry
Sekt	German sparkling wine

Bigger bottles

Magnum	equivalent of 2 standard (750ml) bottles
Jeroboam	equivalent of 4 bottles
Methuselah	equivalent of 8 bottles
Salmanazar	equivalent of 12 bottles
Balthazar	equivalent of 16 bottles
Nebuchadnezzar	equivalent of 20 bottles

Light Wines

AC/AOC	(Appellation d'Origine Contrôlée) French system of wine classification according to strict specifications, including geographical location and grapes
Château-bottled	Wine put in bottles on the estate where it was made
Cosecha	Vintage/crop (Spanish)
Crianza	Spanish red wines with at least two years' ageing
Cru Classé	Any wine from the five Médoc (Bordeaux) classifications
DO	(Denominación de Origen) Spanish classification system
DOCa	(Denominación de Origen Calificada) Superior Spanish wine classification; Rioja is the only current example
DOC/DOCG	(Denominazione de Origine Controllata) Italian system of classification - sometimes has a 'G' (for 'Garantita') added, indicating the highest quality
Gran Reserva	Spanish red wines with at least five years' ageing
Grand Cru	'Great growth', the name given to top-ranking Burgundy wines
Grand Cru Classé	Second ranking wines from St Emilion
Grand Vin	'Great Wine' (French) without any specific classification criteria
Mise en bouteille au château	French for château-bottled
Moelleux	Medium-sweet (French)
Premier Cru	'First growth'; confusingly, second-ranking wines from Burgundy
Premier Cru Classé	Top-ranking wines from the Médoc and Graves in Bordeaux
Deuxième/Troisième/ Quatrième/Cinquième Cru Classé	Four remaining Bordeaux classifications for the Médoc and Graves – historical rather than purely qualitative
Premier Grand Cru Classé	Top-ranking wines from St Emilion
QbA	(Qualitätswein bestimmte Anbaugebiete) Second level of German wines, which may have sugar added before fermentation
QmP	(Qualitätswein mit Prädikat) Top quality German wines, whose natural sugar is sufficient to ensure successful fermentation. Further delineated from driest to sweetest as Kabinett, Spätlese, Auslese, Beerenauslese, Trockenbeerenauslese
Recioto	Italian wine made from semi-dried grapes
Reserva	Spanish red wines with at least three years' ageing
Trocken	Dry (German)
VDQS	(Vins Délimités de Qualité Supérieure) French wines from areas just below AOC status – not frequently used
Vin de Pays	Third down on the scale of French wine classification – but some real gems to be had

Some of your favourite grapes may be hiding from you under a different name. This is most likely with Old World wines, whereas the trend in the New World is to put the grape variety on the bottle, as well as a brand name.

Quaffers® brings the uninitiated a small selection of French wines which may have escaped your attention, despite being made from familiar grapes.

White grapes

GRAPE	APPELLATION
Chardonnay	Burgundy, including Chablis, Meursault, Montrachet, Pouilly-Fuissé etc
Chenin Blanc	Bonnezeaux Côteaux du Layon Savennières Vouvray
Sauvignon Blanc	Ménétou-Salon Pouilly-Fumé Sancerre
Sauvignon Blanc/Sémillon blend	Bordeaux (dry and sweet wines)
Viognier	Château-Grillet Condrieu

Black grapes

GRAPE	APPELLATION
Cabernet Sauvignon/ Cabernet Franc/Merlot blend	Bordeaux, including Graves, Médoc
Gamay	Beaujolais, including Brouilly, Chénas, Chiroubles, Côte de Brouilly, Fleurie, Juliénas, Morgon, Moulin-à-Vent, Regnié, Saint-Amour
Grenache/Mourvèdre/Syrah blend	Châteauneuf-du-Pape Côtes-du-Rhône (Villages) Gigondas
Merlot/Cabernet Franc/ Cabernet Sauvignon blend	St Emilion Pomerol
Pinot Noir	Burgundy, including Côte de Beaune, Côte de Nuits Sancerre
Syrah	Cornas Côte Rôtie Côtes-du-Rhône Crozes-Hermitage Hermitage St Joseph

Nine favourite grapes to try

If you're out for a glass or two of wine, it's hard to escape the Big Four (Sauvignon Blanc, Chardonnay, Cabernet Sauvignon and its blends, Syrah/Shiraz and its blends). These wines dominate the public palate to such an extent that, because people drink what they know, bars stock accordingly.

The Quaffers® team enjoys a glass of any of these four with the best of you, but lest familiarity should breed contempt, often opts for something more adventurous. Luckily, advances are being made on a good many wine lists to accommodate the inquisitive brigade. Here are some of our top suggestions if you are looking to experiment, but want more than just a grape name to guide you.

Albariño

Fresh white wine from Galicia in north-western Spain, touted by many a Sunday supplement as "Chardonnay for the new Millennium". Let's hope not, for that would be diminishing this wonderful grape with a comparison to another variety whose similarity ends with the colour of the fruit. Light and lean, Albariño offers soft fruit (look for peaches) and zesty acidity which stands up well against the gooseberry grassiness of a Sauvignon Blanc. Portuguese Alvarinho (main grape in Vinho Verde) is the same variety.

Chenin Blanc

This white grape is probably the most versatile of all, with the possible exception of Chardonnay. It can make wines which vary from dry to ultra-sweet, from still to sparkling, from examples to be drunk young to some of the great keepers. The grape's naturally high acidity provides the necessary counterpoint for sun-ripened sugar-packed fruit. Chenin Blanc is grown internationally, and in South Africa it is also known as Steen. However it is in the Loire Valley of France where it really comes into its own, with quality wines of all styles produced under individual appellation names.

Gamay (Beaujolais Crus)

If you've ever wondered why the third Thursday in November seems to be a particularly potent day in the supermarket and high street wine calendar, then you're probably susceptible to the frenzy that accompanies the release of Beaujolais Nouveau. It's also the day when French producers nationwide release any newly-bottled wine, but Beaujolais has cornered the market in international publicity. However, we are not talking about that version of Beaujolais, which is extremely young and made simply. Instead we are referring to wine from any of the ten named Beaujolais districts where the tradition of making the Gamay grape into light, refreshing red wines (ideal at lunchtime) has become an art rather than a clever marketing exercise. For the names of these districts, see our guide to grapes in disguise on page 11.

Gewürztraminer

Traditionally the best of these white wines come from Alsace or Germany with a price to match, but the grape is grown widely throughout the world. Lychees are the key smell, along with honeyed spicy richness which follows through in the mouth. The instant reaction of those unfamiliar with the grape is that it's going to be sweet and therefore unpleasant, but this feature is skilfully tempered with acidity which keeps the grape honest. It's worth paying a little extra for a bottle of this wine; it should reward your experimentation handsomely. If you're eating spicy food, Gewürztraminer is the ideal accompaniment.

Malbec

Increasingly associated with Argentine red wine, this grape variety is also the main constituent of many a South-Western French bottle, particularly from Cahors where it must provide at least 70% of the final blend. With a reputation for intrusively hefty tannins (if your mouth dries out when you taste, you've noticed them), this grape has had its detractors in the past. However wine-making techniques have adapted to create full, fruity wines which are ready for drinking younger than previously. Older examples can offer good quality, with the tannins coming into their own in the ageing process.

Pinot Noir

It might surprise you that we are drawing attention to a widely-known grape which many people recognise as the source of red Burgundy, and which is one of the constituents in the blend of many a Champagne. However, Pinot Noir can be easily misinterpreted and consequently overlooked. Drunk young, it smells of red berries and is relatively pale in colour; when it has been allowed to age and mellow (as with the top examples which have created its reputation), it develops savoury aromas and a rich, dark intensity of colour and flavour which can be an acquired taste. Many French Pinot Noirs have traded shamelessly on the grape's glorious potential, but have been either prohibitively expensive or of disappointing quality – or both. With increasing interest from international growers however, Pinot Noir is a grape to watch, with Australia, North-West USA, Chile and New Zealand leading the way.

Riesling

Again, Alsace and Germany are the principal regions for this white grape, but some excellent examples are emerging from other corners of the wine world. Many quaffers are put off by preconceptions of slushy sweetness, but to do so is to underestimate the wine's structure and range of styles. A floral bouquet and steeliness on the palate are tell-tale signs. Older bottles can have a petrol aroma, but don't let that dissuade you! It can be sweet and even sweeter, but carefully-managed acidity counteracts any cloying factor, and the wines are deceptively light-bodied with low percentage alcohol. On the other hand, some examples are dry and restrained. Riesling is the hidden gem of the wine world, requiring patience but delivering endless satisfaction.

Viognier

Starting to gain popularity with growers around the globe, Viognier's spiritual home is the Condrieu appellation in the northern Rhône Valley in France, where high sugar content in the grapes results in quite alcoholic wines. Bottles from here may have you begging with the bank manager, but look out for examples from other locations, such as South Africa and California, to introduce you to the fragrant peachiness of this delicious white wine.

Zinfandel

Synonymous with the Californian wine industry, 'Zin' as it is affectionately known in wine shorthand, is actually the same as the Italian grape Primitivo. It produces fruity red wines, abundant in berry aromas, often with a Christmas pudding finish, and is becoming a more popular international planting in other equally warm regions. Best examples of Zinfandel are from producers who understand the need to keep yields low and exposure to high temperatures at a minimum. 'White Zinfandel' is made from the same grape, but is actually a pale, sweet rosé (or 'blush' in California-speak). Be careful!

How to taste wine

Most people drink wine with only one question in mind: do I enjoy this? Fair enough. The simple yes/no response to that question is usually instinctive, but if you were pushed for reasons why, what would you say?

Appreciating wine is not an exact science, but it does involve more than just the tastebuds, and can be a lot of fun. Here we give you some pointers to enable you to explain why a particular wine appeals to you. Describing smell and taste doesn't seem to come as easily to most of us as describing sights and sounds does, so it takes some practice. Being specific won't turn you into a wine bore, but it will help you to be more precise about your preferences, and hopefully give you greater confidence when choosing a bottle from a wine list or from a shop shelf.

There are plenty of programmes on television where 'experts' demonstrate the art of wine tasting. It may look showy and seem pretentious, but a low-key imitation of their basic actions is a good place to start if there's nobody else to show you what to do.

Pour the wine so it still has room to move in the glass, and can be swirled as necessary. Ideally, you will be tasting wine in a well-lit room with white surfaces against which to examine the contents of your glass. You will have remembered to avoid strong flavours (including coffee, toothpaste, garlic and onions) and not to wear perfume or eau de toilette. However, it's not always possible to enjoy laboratory conditions, and it certainly shouldn't stop you tasting and enjoying the wine!

To resolve part of this dilemma, we suggest you use the blank white inside cover of Quaffers® London as a background for looking at your wine. Consider the wine's appearance (if there is enough light to do so): is it bright and clear? Generally, wines should not be bubbly (unless sparkling) or cloudy. Is the colour what you would expect for a wine of its age? Young reds will be quite purple around the edges, older reds will start to show brown edges instead. Whites are harder to age by appearance, but, if matured in oak barrels, can take on a deeper colour.

Use your nose to breathe in the wine's aromas. You should think about the intensity of the smells: strong or not? Some wines require exposure to air for them to release their bouquet, so you may have to be patient. Further gentle swirling can assist this. At this stage you can start to think about what any smells remind you of. We recommend that you keep your descriptions simple! Over time, you will learn that different grape varieties have typical aromas, and you can pick the grape without having seen the bottle.

Now to the business end of proceedings. Take a small mouthful of wine, hold your head forward and gargle it in the front of the mouth, trying to let some air in if you can. (Practise a few times first with water.) In the normal order of things, sweetness should hit first on the tip of the tongue, followed closely by an awareness of mouth-watering acidity (especially in white wines) or mouth-drying tannins (ageing compound in red wines). Fruit should kick in next, and if the wine is particularly alcoholic, there can be a warming sensation at the back of the mouth.

The lasting impression of the wine after it has been swallowed (or spat out) is known as its 'finish', measured in terms of length: short, medium or long. A longer and more intense finish can indicate a good quality wine.

The combination of all these factors will tell you about the wine's balance and ageing potential, and experience is the best guide for developing such awareness. The beauty of wine-tasting is, that to get better at it, you have to quaff more wine.

So grab Quaffers® London, hit the streets, and keep quaffing!

Knowing whether or not your wine is in good condition is a conundrum which continues to perplex wine drinkers, regardless of knowledge or experience. This can make challenging the staff of a bar or a restaurant an exercise fraught with anxiety and possible embarrassment, which is enough to make many people suffer poor wine in silence.

However, there are rules of thumb which may help you to decide if the wine you are hoping to enjoy is in worse shape than it should be. Fortunately the percentage of obviously duff bottles of wine is relatively small, so the odds are with the buyer.

In the case of wines served by the glass, it's wise to keep your eyes open to see how the bar keeps the bottle from which your wine is poured. Many establishments have invested in sophisticated wine preservation systems which should keep the wine 'fresh', but don't be afraid to ask how long it is since the bottle was first opened. And beware any unstoppered bottles!

Start by checking the bottle to see if the vintage (year) is the same as that listed. Some unscrupulous places try to offload inferior vintages of the same wine on to unsuspecting customers. Many lists now carry a disclaimer which accommodates substitute vintages. As ever – look out for the small print! Remember though, that substitutions are often made for valid reasons – supplies of the listed vintage have been exhausted and a newer one is on the market, or the establishment has not reprinted its wine list yet.

Look at the wine for its colour and clarity. A healthy-looking example will be bright and glossy, whereas a poor one will be dull and lifeless. If you see small crystalline deposits (tartrate crystals) on the cork or in the bottle, this is a natural phenomenon, and is not a bad thing!

Swish the wine in the glass to release the aromas. Hopefully there will be an inkling of fruit, and pleasant hints of all sorts of things, even if the wine needs a bit more air to really show its character. Anything that smells musty or like rotten eggs, sharp vinegar, heavy port, Grandpa's sock drawer or putrid compost is likely to have something wrong with it, and should be politely but firmly refused. Remember that unusual smells (farmyard, forest floor, cat's pee on the infamous gooseberry bush) are not always bad signs. It's when they make you think of unpleasant connotations that you need to be on your guard. If you're still not quite sure, venture a sip. If the wine is in poor condition, some of the nasty things you smelled will also be evident to the taste, as the two senses are closely connected.

'Corked' has to be one of the most familiar yet misunderstood phrases connected with wine. If there are bits of cork floating in your glass, this does not mean it is 'corked', rather that the cork has broken while being extracted. There is unlikely to be anything wrong with the wine, except that it might need straining to remove the offending particles.

As the catch-all cry which is likely to accompany the discovery of any seriously unpleasant defects in wine, "Corked!" is often misleading and unhelpful. The variety of potential wine faults and their indicators is much greater than those attributed to the humble bottle closure. Many of these faults are virtually imperceptible, even to experts. Any venue worth its salt should be happy to taste the wine, discuss the perceived problem, and replace it if you are unhappy, so don't be shy.

On the other hand, there are some real corkers out there just waiting to be tried. Whether you indulge in a full theatrical wine tasting psrformance, or simply cast your eyes, nose and tastebuds over the wine before you, the key question remains: do I enjoy this wine? And the answer, as with the criteria you use to make the final decision, is entirely personal.

Editor's choice

While researching this book, we visited countless wine bars all over London in all weathers, and became very well acquainted with the highways and byways of the city. You can read the results of our quest in the following pages.

Although many of the listed venues possess their own charm and style, there are a handful which really stand out. These are places where there is an intangible 'X-factor' which, time and again, would send us back to the office, exclaiming: "I went to this fantastic bar in London yesterday. You've got to go there!"

Here are our favourites:

Albertine
The Arches
Bleeding Heart Tavern & Bistro
Cork & Bottle
The Crescent
Frederick's
Gordon's
Odette's
Smithy's
Vat's

It goes without saying that each venue in this selection serves an excellent range and quality of wines. What makes them extra special in comparison to many other worthy contenders is down to personal taste and style, but we hope that you will enjoy visiting them, and perhaps create your own 'Top Ten' quaff spots in the capital.

Don't forget to let us know if you have your own favourites, or if you discover a place that we don't yet know about. Contact us at our website **www.quaffers.co.uk** or use the Freepost Business Reply Card at the back of the book.

Cheers!

Mary.

Mary Thurston
editor@quaffers.co.uk

Quaffers London
The venues

Aldgate Colony Wine Bar

48 Aldgate High Street, EC3
☎020 7265 0975
Mon-Fri: 11am - 9pm
14 @ £2.80 - £4.00
56 @ £10.90 - £98.00

Hidden depths

If you happen to be in this area of town, then the Aldgate Colony Wine Bar is a good bet for a decent glass of wine and a bite to eat. A small entrance belies the cavernous depth of the bar, which is filled with functional rather than decorative wooden tables and chairs. Outside is a yard area, which comes into its own on those rare but welcome sunny days. Welcoming staff are polite and friendly, and the wine list offers a good selection of international wines including a small range of fine wines and Champagnes.

The Marine Broker

17 Lehman Street, E1
☎020 7481 1997
Mon-Fri: 11.30am - 9pm
12 @ £2.30 - £3.25
48 @ £8.50 - £28.95

Splice the mainbrace!

An unassuming entrance on the corner of a busy one way street means that The Marine Broker is probably a well-kept secret amongst local residents and office workers. Its small interior, exposed brickwork, wooden floors and attractive traditional bar give a comforting atmosphere in which to sip a glass of wine. The wine list comprises six house whites and reds which are rather basic, but moves on to a more interesting selection by the bottle. Well-known European and New World producers dominate, ensuring that customers will enjoy whichever wine they choose.

Barcelona Tapas Bar & Restaurant

1a Bell Lane, E1
☎020 7247 7014
Mon-Fri: 11am - 11pm
9 @ £2.50 - £4.75
99 @ £9.95 - £125.00

Viva España

This tiny basement bar and restaurant, tucked down a back street in East London, is home to one of the greatest ranges of Spanish wine available in the city. The setting is very simple with stools and counters replacing tables and chairs, and a large servery full of appetising tapas dominating the limited floor space. Although there are few wines available by the glass, those available by the bottle more than compensate. The list is arranged by wine region and the quaffer is given grape and alcohol content information as well as a tasting note to aid choice. An excellent place to explore the breadth of wines Spain has to offer.
www.barcelona-tapas.com

Poet Bar & Brasserie

Cree House, 20 Creechurch Street, EC3
☎020 7623 3999
Mon-Fri: 11am - 11pm
20 @ £2.75 - £5.50
46 @ £10.50 - £115.95

"Wine is bottled poetry" (R.L.Stevenson)

The Poet Bar is easy to spot on a quiet lane just off the eastern end of Leadenhall Street. The bar area is situated at ground level with a separate restaurant in the basement. Staff here are very friendly and this, together with the stripped pine floor, bright paintwork and comfy seating areas (not to mention the large screen televisions), means that you can quickly feel at home. The wine list contains a reasonable range with twenty of the wines offered by the glass. Beware though, no tasting note is offered, nor is the wine's country of origin stated, so brush up on your producers before setting foot in here! A fun quaffing spot for light-hearted wine-lovers.

Plus:

Bill Bentley's (Young's)

5 Minories, EC3
☎020 7481 1779

Corney & Barrow

37 Jewry Street, EC3
☎020 7680 8550

Jamies

Aldgate Barrs, Marsh Centre,
10 Whitechapel High St, E1
☎020 7265 1977

The Duke of Cambridge

30 St Peter's Street, N1
☎020 7359 3066
Mon: 5pm - 11pm; Tue-Sat: 12.30pm - 11pm
Sun: 12.30pm - 10.30pm
14 @ £2.75 - £7.50
46 @ £11.00 - £50.00

Organic gastropub fills a gap

Dominating the corner of St Peter's and Danbury Streets, inside The Duke is like being in a friend's farmhouse kitchen: well-scrubbed, warm and inviting. Blue and cream paintwork, weathered tables and chairs, fresh flowers and daily newspapers add to the homeliness, and the tiny patio courtyard at the back is another feature. People come here to sample the extensive range of organic food and drink, and the place has a mixed clientele. Wines are international and exclusively organic (including vegetarian, vegan and biodynamic), with all products certified by the Soil Association, making The Duke a ground-breaker in London. Sister pubs The Crown in E3, and The Pelican in W11 provide similar fare.
www.singhboulton.co.uk/duke

Frederick's

Camden Passage, N1
☎020 7359 2888
Mon-Sat: 11am - 11pm
23 @ £2.75 - £8.95
146 @ £10.95 - £95.00

Exceptional vintage quality

Follow your nose up Islington High Street from the Tube, keeping your eyes open on the right for Camden Passage. Frederick's is neighbour to the many antique and bric-a-brac emporia lining this lane, which runs parallel to the main road. The bar flows into a beautifully appointed restaurant, and you can even get married here in the pretty garden at the back of the premises. All is style and elegance, with wines to match which have been selected by the 82 year-old owner. The venue's policy, stated on the menu, is "to have a reasonably priced wine list, with wines of a consistently high quality, so that our customers can choose and experiment with confidence." Judging by the range of French and international wines on offer, they are true to their word. Unmissable.

Angel

The Social

Arlington Square, N1
020 7354 5809
Mon-Fri: 5pm - 11pm
Sat: 11am - 11pm; Sun: 11am - 10.30pm
12 @ £2.55 - £5.00
22 @ £9.75 - £35.00

Mellow makeover

Formerly the Hanbury Arms, the Social has inherited a fine wine cellar from the previous incumbents, and will offer interesting bottles from it for some time to come. Double reason then to wander into the quiet residential squares beyond the Angel to discover this friendly gastropub on the Linton Street corner of Arlington Square. The '30s-style panelled wood interior has been tastefully refurbished, and despite a surfeit of brown about the place, it has warmth and vitality. Staff describe the menu as "Modern British with a Scottish influence", and the listed wines are international with reliable names included. But it's the specials which will draw you in, so make the most of some genuine treats at excellent prices.

Plus:

All Bar One

1 Liverpool Road, N1
020 7843 0021

Café Med

370 St John Street, EC1
020 7278 1199

Pitcher & Piano

68 Upper Street, N1
020 7704 9974

Archway

St John's Bar & Dining Room

91 Junction Road, N19
020 7272 1587
Mon-Sat: 11am - 11pm
Sun: Noon - 10.30pm
14 @ £2.75 - £4.00
29 @ £11.00 - £27.50

Spread the word!

Not far down the road from the Tube, St John's spans a mini-block and consequently has windows on three sides, letting in masses of light to the spacious bar area and the restaurant at the rear. This is a remodelled pub, but don't let that put you off; it has developed its own style which matches relaxed comfortable surroundings with good quality food and drinks. The restaurant wine list is available in the bar if you ask, but in any case there are fifteen possibilities chalked up above the counter. These include a good range of grapes in an Old World selection which changes relatively frequently. Archway may not be the first place you would look for decent wine, but St John's breaks the mould.

Carpe Diem

28 Paddington Street, W1
☎020 7935 0556
Mon-Fri: 10.30am - 11pm
Sat: Noon - 10pm; Sun: Noon - 5pm
13 @ £2.50 - £5.00
17 @ £9.00 - £40.00

Good for everyone

On the corner of Chiltern Street, and a stone's throw from Madame Tussaud's and the London Planetarium, Carpe Diem is ideal both if you're by yourself or on the move with friends or family. This comfortable pub caters for all tastes, and while the wines owe more to the High Street than to exclusive merchants, there should be something on the list which appeals for a quick drink. The crowd which comes here ranges from tourists to language students to locals, there are papers available to read in quieter moments, and the overall impression is one of warmth and informality.

The Providores

109 Marylebone High Street, W1
☎020 7935 6175
Mon-Fri: 8am - 10.45pm
Sat & Sun: 10am - 10.45pm
26 @ £4.00 - £8.50
48 @ £12.50 - £150.00

Kiwi café culture comes to the capital

The most recently opened of all the venues in this book is a quality addition to the London wine drinking scene. This part of town is thriving again, and the bar, in a former pub, successfully combines old-style premises with modern minimalism. A huge Polynesian tapa cloth hangs on the wall opposite the bar, and there is seating at a high central bench, in the bow window, or on a long banquette. The owners have created a sophisticated yet comfortable venue where you can chill out alone or with friends, and profit from an excellent wine list which boasts twenty-two New Zealand bottles plus some unusual international classics. It's on the pricey side, but the original fusion of food, drink and laid-back Antipodean atmosphere merits a visit.
www.theprovidores.co.uk

Suze Wine Bar

1 Glentworth Street, NW1
☎020 7486 8216
Mon-Fri: Noon - 11pm
14 @ £2.75 - £4.95
64 @ £10.50 - £120.00

Flying Kiwi

There is a corner of a foreign capital which is forever New Zealand, at least as far as wine is concerned, and this is it. The Montana awning just off the north side of the Marylebone Road signals Suze to the world, and inside there are plenty of visuals to bring the Antipodes to life. Friendly Kiwi management and staff can tell you about the wines and recommend a dish from the menu. Two cosy bar areas are the ideal setting to enjoy one of the vast range of New Zealand vintages, including many of the top producers. Chardonnay is a speciality, but all the other favourites are listed too. Look out for Suze's sister restaurant-bar in Mayfair too.

Plus:

All Bar One

7-9 Paddington Street, W1
☎020 7487 0071

Dock Blida (Davy's)

50-54 Blandford Street, W1
☎020 7486 3590

Balham

Macnab's Wine Bar & Restaurant

43 Balham High Road, SW12
020 8675 5522
Mon-Sat: 11am - 11pm
Sun: 11am - 10.30pm
6 @ £2.40 - £3.50
33 @ £9.95 - £39.50

Balham bonus

On the main road to the north of both the Tube and railway stations, Macnab's waves the flag for wine in this part of South London. A raised terrace lifts the clientele off the arterial traffic route which is the High Road, and provides an oasis of relative calm. Inside is a comfortable dining and drinking area, bistro-style, with '30s French posters, plants and mirrors to enhance the scene. The manager is aiming to extend the range of the wine list, but for the moment its eclectic choice concentrates on some top producers from both Old and New Worlds. There is also a specials board which changes weekly.

Plus:

The Duke of Devonshire (Young's)

39 Balham High Road, SW12
020 7673 1363

The Grove (Young's)

39 Oldridge Road, SW12
020 8673 6531

Bank

Lay & Wheeler Wine Bar

33 Cornhill, EC3
020 7626 0044
Mon-Fri: 11am - 10pm
23 @ £2.95 - £7.75
96 @ £11.50 - £199.00

First Class

Owned by the eponymous wine merchants and located just up from the busy intersection at Bank, this bar is a quaffer's haven. The décor is tastefully simple with stripped pine floors and pine furniture, adding to the bar's airy modern feel. The wine list includes a separate section devoted to both red and white fine wines, and displays a sparkling array of top producers from both the Old and New Worlds. Curious quaffers might like to experiment with one or two of the wines made from more unusual grapes. Though catering mainly for the City crowd, this is nevertheless a top spot for any wine-lover.

Bank

Options

1 Angel Court, 30 Throgmorton Street, EC2
☎020 7600 4220
Mon-Fri: 11am - 11pm
9 @ £2.85 - £3.75
30 @ £10.50 - £45.00

Take your pick!

Options couldn't be closer to the London Stock Exchange, making it a popular choice with local traders and support staff. Brass handrails on a staircase of '80s vintage establish a vaguely nautical feel, followed up by portholed swing doors into the main bar. Inside it seems like the lounge of an ocean liner; whether this is intentional remains a mystery! Considering its prime location, Options does not abuse the wallet, and both food and drinks are rationally priced. The wine list concentrates on France but includes other countries for some balance. This part of London is full of possibilities for refreshment; Options offers a fairly traditional approach to the basic steak-and-wine bar formula, although it only does food at lunchtimes.

Room Café Bar ⊖

10 Copthall Avenue, EC2
☎020 7374 4666
Mon-Fri: 11am - 11pm
5 @ £2.10 - £5.65
27 @ £8.35 - £135.00

Unusual blend

Approaching from London Wall, keep an eye out on the left hand side of the street, as it's easy to walk past Room Café Bar's unprepossessing exterior. Inside, the pale green and silver room is home to an eclectic mix of wall sculpture and art, all in an '80s style bar setting. The large bar is towards the back, and there is plenty of seating. Wines are mainly French, although there are some international choices too. If you want to come here just for a drink, the list will no doubt contain something of interest. With the bar menu featuring dishes from the Indian sub-continent, matching one of these wines may be more problematic, so you need a spirit of adventure.

Plus:

All Bar One
34 Threadneedle Street, EC2
☎020 7614 9931

Balls Brothers
King's Arms Yard, EC2
☎020 7796 3049

Corney & Barrow
111 Old Broad Street, EC2
☎020 7638 9308

Corney & Barrow
16 Royal Exchange, EC2
☎020 7929 3131

Jamies
54 Gresham Street, EC2
☎020 7606 1755

Number 25 (Jamies)
25 Birchin Lane, EC3
☎020 7623 2505

Pitcher & Piano
28-30 Cornhill, EC3
☎020 7929 3989

Cellar Gascon ⊖

59 West Smithfield, EC1
☎020 7796 0600
Mon-Fri: Noon - Midnight
Sat: 5pm - Midnight
🍷21 @ £2.50 - £7.00
🍾72 @ £10.00 - £120.00

South-West France comes into its own

For all things South-Western, don't walk past Cellar Gascon; unless you are going to their restaurant next door, or get waylaid by their deli at Comptoir Gascon nearby. The bar oozes cool but has a warm Gallic welcome for those remotely interested in discovering this region. A funky map on the end wall gives a geographical perspective to what you are enjoying; sausages hang curing behind the bar, and 19th century leather rugby balls recall the gastronomic and sporting traditions which are still strong today. The native staff are passionate about their region, shown in their willingness to suggest something new or different from the wide range of exclusively South-Western wines. Wines can also be purchased on an off-licence basis. Be in early to get a table – otherwise join the happy scrum standing beside the bar.

Laine's Wine Bar

13-17 Long Lane, EC1
☎020 7726 8858
Mon-Fri: Noon - 8pm
🍷5 @ £2.50 -£4.90
🍾28 @ £10.50 - £43.50

Old school tradition

If you yearn for a traditional City wine drinking scenario, then Laine's is the place to come. Down some stairs past wine-related quotes, paintings and other memorabilia, you find yourself in a long underground room with a bar at one end and a smart dining area at the other. Tables and chairs are dotted about, it's well-lit, but piped crooners and subdued paint shades speak of another era. The wine list is mainly French and Italian, including some bottles from mid-'90s vintages, rather than concentrating solely on later years as in most places. This is unreconstructed old-school wine bar territory, with the focus on drinking wine by the bottle over a business lunch, or dropping in with colleagues on the way home.

Mustard's Smithfield Brasserie

60 Long Lane, EC1
☎020 7796 4920
Mon-Fri: Noon - 11pm
🍷10 @ £2.50 - £4.95
🍾53 @ £10.50 - £200.00

Claret drinkers well served

The owner of Mustard's has a vineyard in South-West France, and the snug brasserie has walls lined with old French signs and wine posters. Tables and chairs are cheek by jowl, with candles and tablecloths adding to the bistro effect. Friendly helpful staff will bring you predominantly French wines, with a few well-chosen New World counterparts such as Wolf Blass, Grange and Trinity Hill. Mustard's is perfectly situated for a good value drink or dinner before attending a weekday performance in the Barbican Centre up the road, but locals are also in the know and keep the brasserie, and its sister restaurant next door, packed out in the evenings.

Plus:

Betjeman's (Jamies)

44 Cloth Fair, EC1
☎020 7600 7778

Jamies ⊖

64-66 West Smithfield, EC1
☎020 7600 0700

Berries

167 Queen Victoria Street, EC4
☎020 7329 4759
Mon-Fri: 11am - 9pm
8 @ £2.75 - £3.75
49 @ £10.80 - £45.00

Hidden fruit

Berries is tucked away in an underground cellar just by Blackfriars station. It has quite an atmospheric setting with wooden floors, old pictures and dusty old bottles adorning the crevices, and the wine list is both extensive and eclectic. There is also a cellar of fine wines, where customers can choose a bottle from the selection and have it opened at their table. A cute little bar which definitely merits a visit, but as there are few wines available by the glass you either need to have a good thirst or should take along a friend or two!

Blackfriars

Drakes Wine Bar

62 Carter Lane, EC4
☎020 7248 4220
Mon-Fri: 11.30am - 11pm
11 @ £2.80 - £4.95
33 @ £10.95 - £48.50

Local flavour

Drakes is not far from St Paul's Cathedral, and is off the beaten track of both City workers and tourists alike. This basement bar has the atmosphere of a 'local' pub with friendly staff, pool table and lingering smells from the subterranean kitchens. Pockets of seating are to be found throughout the space and, despite the rather smoky air, it has a certain appeal. The wine list is sensible, with a good range of grapes and recent vintages at reasonable prices. In particular, house wines offer good value for money.

⊖ ⇌ Blackfriars

La Grande Marque

47 Ludgate Hill, EC4

☎020 7329 6709

Mon-Fri: 11.30am - 11pm

22 @ £3.50 - £8.50

101 @ £11.95 - £290.00

Heaven on earth

In the world of London bars, La Grande Marque is something special. The cosy venue on Ludgate Hill is full of City types and has a quiet yet energetic buzz. This place oozes class, from the elaborate ceiling and wood panelling to the choice of wines available. There are effectively three lists here: one for wines offered by the glass, one for bottled wines and one for fine wines. And they do mean fine – La Tâche, Domaine Romanée-Conti, Château Palmer, and Château d'Yquem to name but a few of the fabulous selection offered. However, those without large disposable incomes are also welcome, as the full range has something for everyone. If you love wine, if you have something to celebrate, or if you simply happen to be in the area, time in this temple of wine will be well-spent.

Plus:

All Bar One

44-46 Ludgate Hill, EC4

☎020 7653 9901

Corney & Barrow

3 Fleet Place, EC4

☎020 7329 3141

Davy's at Creed Lane

10 Creed Lane, EC4

☎020 7236 5317

El Vino

30 New Bridge Street, EC4

☎020 7236 4534

Jamies

34 Ludgate Hill, EC4

☎020 7489 1938

Bond Street

Auberge

6 St Christopher's Place, W1

☎020 7486 5557

Mon-Sun: Noon - 11pm

16 @ £2.35 - £3.95

24 @ £9.95 - £49.95

Shelter from the storm

It might be hard to believe, but right behind Oxford Street lies a quiet haven of peace and tranquillity in St Christopher's Place. Auberge is actually in a lane at the back of the small square, leading to Wigmore Street. Pavement tables and azure blue chairs announce Auberge among the other cafés and restaurants around it, and add to the continental flavour of the area. There is also a downstairs bar which is open in the evenings (Tuesday to Saturday). Wines are international and described briefly on the list. If you have reached the dropping part of shopping, Auberge is just the place to put your feet up without adding too much to the cost of your retail therapy.

The Loop

19 Dering Street, W1

☎020 7493 1003

Mon-Sat: Noon - Midnight

10 @ £2.85 - £5.95

19 @ £9.95 - £85.00

West End tardis

The Loop can be found on the corner of Dering Street and Tenterden Street. A small, loud top bar gives way to cavernous bars below ground, complete with dance floor and restaurant. This is a trendy late night haunt for those with stamina and a taste for loud music. During Happy Hour (5pm-7pm) all bottles of wine are half price and Champagne is £10 cheaper. The wine list is basic with a good selection of wines to suit most palates. Plenty of cocktails and designer beer to quench the thirst make this venue ideal for a group with differing tastes.

Suze in Mayfair

41 North Audley Street, Mayfair, W1
☎020 7491 3237
Mon-Sat: 11am - 11pm
🍷20 @ £2.65 - £4.95
🍾80+ @ £10.50 - £55.50

Bar of the long Kiwi list

Suze (and its sister bar at Baker Street Tube) presents itself as London's speciality New Zealand wine bar, and the excellent Kiwi selection bears this out. Wines from Australia also feature strongly. Owners Tom and Susan Glynn have been in London for 25 years, and give a warm Antipodean welcome to all comers. Suze looks like a restaurant from the front, but take the plunge and head to the back where a comfortable bar area allows you to relax and enjoy some really fine wines. Whether you just have a drink, or are tempted to stay for some of the delicious-sounding Pacific Rim menu, this is definitely the place to come in this part of London – and is well worth the effort from further afield.

Plus:

All Bar One

5-6 Picton Place, W1
☎020 7487 0161

Balls Brothers

34 Brook Street, W1
☎020 7499 4567

Basement 92 (Davy's)

92 Wigmore Street, W1
☎020 7224 0170

Delancey Restaurant Bar Café

3 Delancey Street, NW1
☎020 7387 1985
Mon-Sat: 9am - Midnight
Sun: 9am - 10.30pm
🍷4 @ £3.00 - £6.85
🍾17 @ £10.50 - £40.00

Camden chic

Just off Camden High Street, Delancey is a bistro-style warren of alcoves and spaces where customers can partake of Gallic fare served up by staff clad in typical garçon manner. Fresh flowers on the tables, occasional wall art and generally unpretentious décor maintain a laid-back bohemian ambience, and in summer this spills from French windows onto the pavement outside. If you weren't already convinced of its cross-Channel credentials, the diva belting out French torch songs on the stereo will provide the final proof. Although the wine list is not extensive, it has a decent regional selection of French wines and a couple of Chilean bottles to add variety.

Plus:

The Spread Eagle (Young's)

141 Albert Street, NW1
☎020 7267 1410

Canary Wharf

Nicolas Bar à Vins

Unit 480, 1 Canada Square, E14
☎020 7512 9092
Mon-Fri: 11am - 8pm
Sat: 11am - 5pm
19 @ £1.50 - £5.00
100+ from £4.99

A votre santé!

Situated under Canary Wharf tower in the shopping malls of the metropolis to the east of the City, this is the first UK Bar à Vins opened by the Nicolas wine merchant chain. There are twenty-five similar bars in France, and hopefully many more will open before long on this side of the Channel. The bar is attached to the Nicolas wine shop; customers can select a glass of wine from the menu, or choose a bottle from the shop shelf to be opened there and then. ISO standard tasting glasses are used, so while measures are smaller than usual, the ability to see, smell and taste the wine should be greatly enhanced. Bottles are charged at normal retail price with no corkage charge added. The wine and food menu changes every three weeks, with reasonably-priced dishes accompanied by a wine recommendation.

Plus:

All Bar One
42 Mackenzie Walk, South Colonnade, E14
☎020 7513 0911

Corney & Barrow
9 Cabot Square, E14
☎020 7512 0397

Davy's at Canary Wharf
31-35 Fisherman's Walk, E14
☎020 7363 6633

The Fine Line
10 Cabot Square, E14
☎020 7513 0255

Jamies
Canary Riverside, 28 Westferry Circus, E14
☎020 7536 2861

The City Page

2a Suffolk Lane, EC4
☎020 7626 0996
Mon-Fri: 11am - 9pm
11 @ £2.95 - £4.95
56 @ £11.95 - £160.00

Pin stripes & cigars

The City Page is hidden away on a quiet corner a short distance from the main thoroughfare, so keep your eyes peeled. This is a typical City wine bar that is roomy but feels cosy at the same time. The wine list is long and arranged by name rather than varietal or price. Its focus is on Champagne, top growth Claret and Burgundy, plus fine wines from the New World. Wines offered by the glass are familiar and solid but less exciting than the main list. As with the other "Page" bars hidden in quiet streets across the capital, this is a good quaffing zone!

www.frontpagepubs.com

Drakes Wine Bar

5 Abchurch Yard, EC4
☎020 7623 2355
Mon-Fri: 11.30am - 11pm
8 @ £2.80 - £3.50
33 @ £10.95 - £40.80

Worth a gander!

The yard is situated off Abchurch Lane, a few steps from Cannon Street station. This basement City bar offers thirsty office workers a good standard array of wines, served in a friendly, busy atmosphere. Nooks and crannies are filled with bars and stools, and one section of the available space is cordoned off for those wishing to eat. Not for the discerning wine buff, but great for a reliable quaff in traditional surroundings.

Plus:

All Bar One

103 Cannon Street, EC4
☎020 7220 9031

The Lansdowne

90 Gloucester Avenue, NW1
020 7483 0409
Mon-Sat: Noon - 11pm
Sun: Noon - 10.30pm
8 @ £2.80 - £3.50
18 @ £11.50 - £32.00

Traditional but in no way twee

This large corner gastropub is a real gem, inevitably refurbished but retaining much of the relaxed character of its former guise. Here you will find a roomy drinking space with big windows and high ceilings, navy and cream paintwork, and comfortable weathered furniture. The Lansdowne offers an excellent range of interesting drinks, all chalked up on boards around the room. However you will find "nothing that goes into a cocktail", as one staff member put it, which more or less sets out the Lansdowne's beverage policy. While the wines may be relatively few, what there is has been extremely well-chosen, mostly from the Old World. This is the perfect place to enjoy a couple of glasses before heading for Primrose Hill or Regent's Park.

Odette's Restaurant & Wine Bar

130 Regent's Park Road, NW1
020 7586 5486/020 7586 8766
Mon-Sat: 12.30 - 3pm/5.30pm - 11pm
Sun: 12.30pm - 3pm
24 @ £3.15 - £6.75
105 @ £11.95 - £190.00

Magnifique!

Amongst the Primrose Hill shops across the canal from the Tube, Odette's is an iconoclast on the London wine scene. Split into a restaurant at street level (walls bedecked with gilt-framed mirrors, making the tiny space seem much bigger), a conservatory at the back, and a wine bar downstairs, it provides an ambience for every occasion. The wine bar itself opens in the evenings, and is full of vinous memorabilia and French posters of all sorts, with a couple of snug alcoves hidden away for a more intimate setting. The wine selection is truly impressive, containing not just French and New World classics, but bottles from more obscure international regions too.

Cort's Bar & Restaurant

84-86 Chancery Lane, WC2
020 7405 3349
Mon-Fri: 11.30am - 11pm/2am
15 @ £2.70 - £6.00
76 @ £9.95 - £125.00

Proud independent

Downstairs towards the northern end of the road, Cort's covers a huge space which has been divided into three rooms. The main bar area is fairly traditional, with a long wooden bar, tables and chairs, and tongue and groove timber on the walls. Although all tastes are catered for, wine is clearly a speciality. The international list is supplemented by specials and featured producers, bringing the total available close to the century mark. Depending on the night of the week, there is likely to be some kind of activity going on, such as dance classes or a regular disco (hence the late licence). Luckily the configuration of the rooms allows patrons to sit out of these events to enjoy their wine in a slightly more peaceful corner of the bar!

Hodgson's Wine Bar

115 Chancery Lane, WC2
020 7404 5027
Mon-Fri: Noon - 11pm
17 @ £2.60 - £6.00
52 @ £9.95 - £94.95

Style near the Strand

Underneath its sister restaurant towards the Strand end of Chancery Lane, Hodgson's fills high-ceilinged cellar space with understated elegance. Tables are spread throughout a series of arched alcoves, and there are a couple of small function rooms cleverly integrated into the layout. Fresh flowers and white paint keep the basement light and bright. Service is friendly and efficient, and the wine selection is impressive: listed by varietal with some blended bottles appended. A food servery next to the bar counter provides sustenance – the menu changes daily. Hodgson's is refined and stylish, well worth an excursion if you don't already frequent this part of the capital.

Chancery Lane

Holborn Colony Wine Bar

33 Brooke Street, EC1

☎020 7430 0677

Mon-Fri: 9.30am - 11pm

12 @ £2.70 - £3.90

54 @ £10.50 - £95.00

Vinous content beats decorative style

Hidden down Brooke Street to the side of the red-brick Prudential Building, you could be forgiven for thinking the Colony was part of an office block. Tinted glass windows belie a buzzing interior, absolutely packed at lunchtime with a mixed crowd of City workers, and even babes-in-arms. The décor can only be described as 'traditional '80s wine bar', but this does not detract from an excellent international choice of wines and tasty-looking food. The bar is long with plenty of places to sit, some screens to separate areas, and lighting just the right side of intimate. A great venue for groups; on our visit everyone was having a whale of a time and wasn't remotely interested in returning to work. That sort of feel-good factor is hard to beat!

Rez's Café Bar

14 Fulwood Place, High Holborn, WC1

☎020 7242 4864

Mon-Fri: 9am - 11pm

11 @ £2.75 - £4.00

17 @ £9.50 - £40.00

Hidden extra

You would never know Rez's was here unless you worked locally or we sent you. At the far end of one of the alleys which dart off the north side of High Holborn, this comfortable café-bar holds a warm welcome. Décor is a mellow yellow, the menu has an Italian bent, and wines cover Western Europe and the Americas. There is nothing from Australasia, which makes Rez's relatively unusual in London at the time of writing! This is a place which does the basics well, exists to serve a wide clientele, has no pretensions, and prospers as a result.

Plus:

Bottlescrue (Davy's)

Bath House, 53-60 Holborn Viaduct, EC1

☎020 7248 2157

Chez Gérard

119 Chancery Lane, WC2

☎020 7405 0290

Bacchanalia ⊖

1a Bedford Street, WC2
☎020 7836 3033
Mon-Sat: 11am - 11pm
16 @ £2.50 - £5.25
36 @ £8.95 - £48.50

Contrast to nearby Covent Garden

This basement venue is one of the last bastions of old-style bar in this part of London. The manager is a gent in a suit, and many of his customers fit the same bill. A long wooden bar covers one side of a spacious room, and Toulouse-Lautrec/Belle Epoque prints hang on the walls. The management emphasises a "personal interest in all the wines on offer", and indeed there is adequate international coverage of both Old and New World. While there are no hidden treasures to be found, it's good to know that places like Bacchanalia still have a part to play in feeding and watering the West End.

Gordon's Wine Bar ⊖

47 Villiers Street, Strand, WC2
☎020 7930 1408
Mon-Sat: 11am - 11pm
21 @ £2.80 - £4.00
41 @ £9.25 - £49.95

London institution

In the same family for three generations, Gordon's prides itself on having resisted the urban development encroaching from all sides. It's easy to miss the tiny door in an unprepossessing shop front, and going down the narrow stairs you could be forgiven for thinking you were in the wrong premises. The alternative entrance on the corner near Victoria Gardens doesn't have the same Dickensian charm! Downstairs you are greeted by tables and chairs of ancient provenance crammed into every available space around corners and under railway arches, with candles to light the way. There is absolutely no pretence here, just good old-fashioned value and service. Some interesting wines grace a broad international list, fortified wines take a strong part in proceedings and the food is also excellent. Not to be missed.

The Portrait Restaurant & Bar

National Portrait Gallery
St Martin's Place, WC2
☎020 7312 2490
Sat-Wed: 10am - 5pm
Thu & Fri: 10am - 8.30pm
19 @ £3.20 - £7.00
56 @ £12.50 - £110.00

Face value

Blessed by another of London's great elevated outlooks, The Portrait makes it easy for its clientele to enjoy the view, with picture windows across the whole expanse of the room. The summit of Nelson's Column is virtually at eye-level, and several other landmarks dot the horizon. The venue is on the top floor of the gallery, reached by lift, or by wandering past the fascinating array of faces lining the walls. At lunchtime it's possible to enjoy a drink at the bar, but after 3pm, and on late-opening days part of the seating area becomes available to non-diners. The style is modern and minimalist, with black and chrome fittings offset by fresh flowers. Nothing detracts from the panorama outside. Wines cover a familiar range of grapes from international sources, mostly of recent vintage, and appealing to every palate.

Plus:

Champagne Charlie's (Davy's) ⊖
17 The Arches, Villiers Street, WC2
☎020 7930 7737

Pitcher & Piano ⊖
40-42 William IV Street, WC2
☎020 7240 6180

Tappit Hen (Davy's) ⊖
5 William IV Street, WC2
☎020 7836 9839

Babel

3-7 Northcote Road, SW11
020 7801 0043
Mon-Sat: 11am - 11pm
Sun: Noon - 10.30pm
5 @ £2.90 - £5.50
23 @ £11.50 - £125.00

Clapham Junction cool

Any connection with the biblical tower is tenuous, unless the constant chat that emanates from customers is what one is supposed to discern from the name. A wide, spacious area has its bar at the back, leaving plenty of room for soft sofas, low stools, and easy chairs, plus tables indoors and out. The '70s-style autumnal paintwork is geometric, producing a soothing overall effect for drinkers and diners alike. Wines are mostly European in origin, with a few from Chile or South Africa to make up the numbers. This is a great place for groups to come to share a bottle or two, given its reasonable prices, and there is a real buzz in the evenings and at weekends.

Le Bar des Magis

5-9 Battersea Rise, SW11
020 7238 0307
Mon-Sat: 10am - 11pm
Sun: 10am - 10.30pm
7 @ £3.25 - £5.40
14 @ £11.95 - £62.00

France without crossing the Channel

Imagine you live in a small French town. Imagine you like popping into one of the local bars with friends, to chat or perhaps to watch the football or rugby team in its latest match. While there, you can have some snacks and a glass from the adequate selection of French wines, knowing that a full restaurant list is also available for the asking. Seats are either at small high tables where you can perch on wooden stools, on the terrace in bright sunshine, or on comfortable sofas and armchairs. Now imagine that you can do all this in London: and you have Le Bar des Magis (and its sister establishment, Le Bar du Lyonnais, in nearby Queenstown Road, SW8). Formidable!

BarCoast

281 Lavender Hill, SW11
020 7924 8021
Mon-Fri: Noon - 11pm
Sun: Noon - 10.30pm
9 @ £2.30 - £2.70
15 @ £9.50 - £50.00

Decent wine not forgotten

Not far from the railway station, BarCoast occupies an unusual triangular site which gives it an aerodynamic look. Its vivid interior paint job doesn't immediately suggest great sophistication, yet the wine list comprises both industry standards and finer examples at affordable prices. These can be enjoyed at one of the tables, or in the plush sofas in a quieter corner of the space. BarCoast is for young drinkers out on the town, so don't come here in the evenings unless you're up for loud music and a big crush. During the day it's much calmer, and the good news is that wine drinkers won't draw a short straw whenever they choose to visit.

Ditto ≹

55-57 East Hill, Wandsworth, SW18
☎020 8877 0110
Mon-Fri: Noon - 11pm
Sat: 10.30am - 11pm; Sun: 10.30am - 10pm
13 @ £2.85 - £8.75
59 @ £11.50 - £87.95

Twice as nice

Strictly speaking, this bar is nearer Wandsworth Town railway station, but the walk up from the Junction along St John's Hill is far more straightforward. Ditto is split in two, bar on one side and more formal restaurant on the other, but the theme throughout is comfort, calm and quiet cool. The menu recommends being "bold, brave and different" by turning off the mobile and giving everybody the chance to leave the modern world outside for a while. This sums up the altruistic approach at Ditto. Wines are international, with curiosities for those who like to try more unusual grapes such as Terret, Malbec, Pinot Blanc and Pinotage, and there is an impressive selection of fine wines too.

The Holy Drinker

59 Northcote Road, SW11
☎020 7801 0544
Mon-Fri: 4.30pm - 11pm
Sat: Noon - 11pm; Sun: 1pm - 10.30pm
5 @ £2.90 - £3.75
21 @ £11.00 - £115.00

Independent original

Fast becoming an institution among Clapham Junction wine-lovers, the Holy Drinker gets most of its treasures from near-neighbour merchants Philglas & Swigot. The discerning blackboard list changes frequently, making every visit to this curious den a pleasure. The manager knows his subject, and can advise customers if they wish to try something new. Unlike most bars, the Holy Drinker doesn't serve food, although that's not a problem in a street lined with eateries of all sorts. This is the place to come for reliable wines to enjoy in a low-key, laid-back environment. And if your friends prefer real ales, they will be happy to join you here too.

Hydro

137-139 St John's Hill, SW11
☎020 7924 6167
Mon-Fri: 4pm - Midnight
Sat & Sun: 10am - Midnight
6 @ £2.50 - £3.00
19 @ £9.50 - £95.00

New kid on the block

The newest arrival on the burgeoning St John's Hill bar scene, Hydro is all Miami pastels, neon effects and bubbling water sculptures. Fluffy-framed mirrors add to the mix, hanging above sofas, wall benches and bar stools. French windows across the double-fronted bar open out onto the wide pavement in warm weather. Yet in all this space the bar itself doesn't take up much room, which might make getting a drink on a busy night more of a challenge than you really want it to be. The wine list contains reliable international quaffs, including some well-known brands, so Hydro is clearly looking to establish its credentials before striking out on a more adventurous path.

Joe's Bar & Restaurant

33 Lavender Hill, SW11
☎020 7228 2960
Mon-Fri: 6pm - 11pm
Sat: Noon - 11pm; Sun: Noon - 10.30pm
12 @ £2.50 - £3.95
21 @ £9.95 - £18.95

Iconoclastic local treasure

Close to the Queenstown Road junction, Joe's does its own thing by ignoring the upsurge in generic bars now populating London. A continenal pavement terrace (with awning) introduces a brick-lined interior, the walls crammed with black and white paparazzi shots of the rich and famous, and an unusual mural in an alcove at the back. Should conversation dry up, these provide a ready source of inspiration. The wine list is chalked up on boards, with some bottles changing as often as weekly, and the range is nothing short of eclectic (with a New World emphasis). Joe's would not be out of place in the West End or on Broadway, but the prices are pure South London, i.e. excellent value.

www.joeswinebar.com

≹Clapham Junction

The Lavender

171 Lavender Hill, SW11
☎020 7978 5242
Mon-Fri: Noon - 11pm
Sat: 10.30am - 11pm; Sun: 10.30am - 10.30pm
7 @ £2.15 - £5.50
22 @ £8.50 - £30.00

Purple patch

Patrons of Battersea Arts Centre, opposite The Lavender, can drop in here after a show to enjoy a drop from a solid international wine selection: no great surprises but no major disappointments either. On a corner, large windows let in masses of light during the day. Wooden tables and chairs collected from different sources fill the bar section at the front and continue into the eating area at the back. The Lavender gets busy in the evenings, especially as the weekend approaches, so it's wise to book if you want a table. Standing space is limited. Food is tasty, staff are helpful, and the lavender theme is not overplayed, beyond the basic wall colour (and the manager's shirt-and-tie combination when we visited).

The Quarry Bar

140 St John's Hill, SW11
☎020 7738 9089
Mon-Fri: Noon - 11pm
Sat: 10.30am - 11pm
Sun: 10.30am - 10.30pm
8 @ £2.50 - £5.00
24 @ £9.95 - £43.00

All things to all people

Sitting on a sunny corner, this friendly spot is decked out in lilac and lavender, with quarry tile floor and unusual verdigris touches behind the copper-clad bar. It offers relaxed eating and drinking, in the light airy main room, at pavement tables, or in a small courtyard at the rear. The wine list presents plenty of geographical and vinification detail, as well as the more usual flavour descriptions, and the international selection is offered at realistic prices. The Quarry does more or less everything you could wish for in both food and drink, making it a popular location for those who venture south of the river.

Plus:

All Bar One

32-38 Northcote Road, SW11
☎020 7801 9951

The Fine Line

31-37 Northcote Road, SW11
☎020 7924 7387

The Front Room

45 Lavender Hill, SW11
☎020 7738 1879

Pitcher & Piano

94 Northcote Road, SW11
☎020 7738 9781

 Covent Garden

Le Bar des Amis du Vin

11-14 Hanover Place, WC2
020 7379 3444
Mon-Sat: 11.30am - 11pm
19 @ £2.75 - £5.70
55 @ £10.95 - £59.95

Friend for life

Below the Café des Amis in a tiny square near the Royal Opera House, this basement bar is a hidden gem in the tourist trap that is Covent Garden. A mixed clientele of all ages comes here to get away from the hustle and bustle outside, happy to sit peacefully on one of the banquettes or low stools placed around a central rectangular bar. Theatrical stills and posters line the walls, spotlit by subtle lighting. The manager has been dispensing wine, cheese and wisdom here for twenty-one years, as regulars will attest. For an excellent range of French wines (with some international bottles and specials listed for good measure) at prices which won't make you faint, Bar des Amis is a great place to know about.
www.cafedesamis.co.uk

Chez Gérard at the Opera Terrace

The Market, Covent Garden, WC2
020 7379 0666
Mon-Sat: 11am - 11pm
Sun: Noon - 10.30pm
15 @ £2.70 - £5.20
31 @ £9.95 - £125.00

Location, location, location!

The Chez Gérard chain has infiltrated all sorts of prime spots in central London, and this is no exception. Situated above the eastern end of the covered market, the Opera Terrace has an excellent vantage point looking out at the Royal Opera House. There is a restaurant in one half and a bar in the other, with the terrace itself running across the front of all of it. Conservatory glass fills the space with light, and at night the view of lit-up surrounding buildings is magical. Chez Gérard is well-known for its French brasserie menu, steak-frites a speciality, and the wine list reflects this Gallic influence. The overall combination of location, food and wine is hard to beat.
www.santeonline.co.uk

The Corner Store

33 Wellington Street, WC2
020 7836 2944
Mon-Fri: 10am - 11pm
Sat: 11am - 11pm; Sun: 11am - 10.30pm
22 @ £2.90 - £8.00
29 @ £10.50 - £50.00

Recent addition to Theatreland

Newly refurbished, the Corner Store has all the elements of modern gastropub that you would expect: wooden tables and chairs, leather sofas and banquettes, substantial bar with brass tap fittings, all with that modern patina of freshly-minted age. Tall windows let in light but start high enough up to afford some privacy to customers. However, its excellent location (on the fringes of Covent Garden near the Lyceum Theatre) helps to overcome any contempt which may result from these over-familiar aspects. The wine list plays safe and concentrates mainly on well-known mid-range international brands, but it's a bonus to have so many of them available by the glass.

Covent Garden

Covent Garden Brasserie

1 & 2 The Piazza, Covent Garden, WC2
☎020 7240 6654
Mon-Sun: 10am - 11pm
13 @ £2.50 - £3.95
35 @ £9.95 - £29.95

Bustling bar for watching buskers

The terrace of this brasserie is just as popular as inside, even in winter. Under the arcades on one side of the Piazza, space heaters keep it warm and shelter is provided by the stone vaulting. The buzzing cosmopolitan vibe of Covent Garden's pedestrian zone is accentuated by blackboards welcoming customers in at least five languages, and everyone, from tourist families to art students to passing shoppers, stops here for refreshments. Wines are mostly French but there is adequate representation from the New World to satisfy all palates. Despite what must sometimes be a challenging job requiring the patience of a saint, staff are unstintingly polite and friendly. Reliable and reasonably-priced: you don't need much more than that.

Crusting Pipe

27 The Market, Covent Garden, WC2
☎020 7836 1415
Mon-Sat: 11am - 11pm
Sun: Noon - 6pm
16 @ £2.85 - £5.00
33 @ £11.25 - £49.95

Anyone for opera?

Although a standard Davy's wine bar in many respects – sawdust on the floor, subterranean arches, wine memorabilia – the Crusting Pipe differs in one major way: it has music. Located downstairs in the heart of the covered market, the bar takes full advantage of a plentiful local resource, namely musicians singing or playing for their supper in the courtyard. After ordering a glass or a bottle from the Davy's list, relax and enjoy Mozart, Puccini, Verdi… volume control dependant on if you decide to sit inside or outside the bar at one of the many tables. This proves to be one of the more pleasant busking experiences to which you might be subjected in Covent Garden, so why not give it a try?
www.davy.co.uk

Henry's Café Bar

5-6 Henrietta Street, WC2
☎020 7379 1871
Mon-Fri: 9am - 11pm
Sat: 10am - 11pm; Sun: 10am - 10.30pm
20 @ £2.55 - £4.85
22 @ £9.85 - £90.00

One for all the family

A vast emporium of everything a hungry or thirsty person could desire, Henry's caters for the masses who flock to the attractions of Covent Garden and the West End. There is a place for this kind of up-front no-nonsense food and drink package, and Henry's makes no bones about it. It is particularly good for families or groups because of the range on offer on the menu. The huge room has a '30s feel to it, with potted palms, parquet floors and tiles abounding. The international wine selection is unremarkable, but if your party comprises all ages and tastes, this bar provides the perfect solution to keep everyone happy.

Porter's Bar

16 Henrietta Street, WC2
☎020 7836 6466
Mon-Sat: Noon - 11pm
Sun: Noon - 10.30pm
17 @ £2.60 - £5.75
21 @ £10.75 - £37.95

Perfect place for a quick quaff

A bright, modern interior welcomes customers into Porter's, where besuited local office workers rub shoulders with passersby. As well as the usual bar stools, tables and seats, there are wicker easy chairs which lend the place a more relaxed air. The long slim space is popular with a younger crowd, and live music is offered on some nights. While this is probably not the place for dedicated wine-lovers, Porter's does offer a reasonable selection of international choices which are described on the list. Fine for a thirst-quenching quaff before moving on elsewhere.
www.porters-bar.com

Covent Garden

Vino

Covent Garden Market, WC2
☎020 7379 3252
Mon-Sat: 11.30am - 11pm
Sun: 11.30am - 5pm
8 @ £2.50 - £2.70
16 @ £9.90 - £25.00

Little Italy in the Market

In a cellar underneath the market, Vino is an intimate den of Italian warmth and cheer. White and lavender paint, quarry tiles and pale wood tables and chairs keep it light, and there are various ingredients on the shelves and walls by way of decoration. Just looking at plump garlic braids, infused oils and dried rosemary makes the prospect of pizza or pasta washed down with an Italian wine infinitely appealing. Vino's particular brand of trattoria is modern and unfussy, making it a pleasant alternative to some other Covent Garden venues.

Plus:

All Bar One
19 Henrietta Street, WC2
☎020 7557 7941

The Marquess of Anglesey (Young's)
39 Bow Street, WC2
☎020 7240 3216

Edgware Road

The Street

58 Crawford Street, W1
☎020 7724 4991
Mon-Fri: 11.30am - 11pm
Sat: 10am - 11pm; Sun: 10am - 10.30pm
8 @ £2.75 - £3.85
22 @ £10.50 - £85.00

Laid-back neighbourhood style

Come out of the Chapel Street Tube exit and head for Crawford Street, where this friendly bar stands on the corner with Homer Street. The owner is Moroccan, and this influence is evident throughout: mosaic-topped tables on the pavement and inside, a few becushioned sofas by a roaring fire, blue and yellow paintwork, tiny mirror tiles and North African curios. The Street attracts a mixed crowd from the surrounding area, as well as those who are willing to venture beyond Oxford Street in search of something a little different. Wines are international in scope, offering a reasonable range which will go down well by themselves, or with something from the Moroccan/Mediterranean menu.

Euston (Square)

The Square Wine Bar & Restaurant

26 Tolmers Square, NW1
020 7388 6010
Mon-Fri: Noon - 11pm
11 @ £2.50 - £3.75
47 @ £10.50 - £43.50

Welcome watering hole

Behind the chaos that is Euston Road, Tolmers Square offers unexpected respite, and Young's Brewery has seized the opportunity to feed and water those who come here seeking peace and quiet. The result is a pub and this adjacent wine bar. The latter is an exercise in late '70s/early '80s styling, with mirrored pillars, potted plants and bistro chairs. Theatre posters and images of ballerinas and 19th century ladies hang on the walls. With Young's behind the scenes, the wine is high quality but reasonably priced, with some treats sprinkled throughout the international selection. There's not much for the wine-lover in this part of town, but The Square makes up for it by providing a reliable choice and pleasant surroundings in which to enjoy it.

Plus:

The Square Tavern (Young's)

26 Tolmers Square, NW1
020 7388 6010

Farringdon

Annabella Wine Bar & Restaurant

45 Clerkenwell Road, EC1
020 7251 0175
Mon-Fri: 11.30am - 11.30pm
7 @ £2.25 - £4.25
24 @ £8.95 - £24.00

Authentic Italian specialities

It makes a refreshing change to find some Old World charm in this increasingly trendy neck of the woods, and Annabella's has it in spades. The cosy brick-lined room doubles as bar and restaurant, with friendly staff, bright tablecloths and easy-on-the-ears Italian music setting the scene. Whoever gets there first in the evening dictates whether the emphasis will be on drinking or dining; it's the kind of place that attracts your attention as you walk past the picture windows, then draws you inside in spite of yourself. This relaxed approach sits easily beside a tasty menu and a mainly Italian wine list, with monthly specials adding to the interest. Make the trek (it's near the junction of Clerkenwell Road and St John's Lane) and you won't be disappointed.

The Bleeding Heart Tavern

Bleeding Heart Yard, Greville Street, EC1
020 7404 0333
Mon-Fri: 11am - 11pm
23 @ £2.65 - £5.50
27 @ £10.50 - £79.50

Legendary location and wine list

The owners of this elegantly restored inn (dating from 1746) are partners in New Zealand's Trinity Hill winery, so it's no surprise that their full range is featured on a list which also includes some top international choices. With huge windows, the brick and blood-red painted interior is light yet cosy, a haven from the City hubbub outside. The wooden bar hails from Victorian times and is a feature in itself. The name carries a dark history which can be discovered in the tavern while pondering what to sample next. Staff are welcoming and helpful, there are various delicious food options, and the overall impression is one of wishing that more pubs were like this one: thoroughly civilised and accommodating. For even more wine delights, make a booking for the sister bistro or restaurant in the yard next door.

⊖ ⇌Farringdon

The Carriage House ⊖

53-54 Farringdon Road, EC4
☎020 7353 4446
Mon-Fri: 11am - 11pm
11 @ £2.60 - £2.95
32 @ £9.50 - £29.95

Local staging post

Electric blue paintwork on the outside of the Carriage House greets those who are prepared to walk up from Ludgate Circus to this cosy venue more or less under Holborn Viaduct. Inside, exposed brickwork adds to the homely atmosphere, and there are photos of the regulars pinned on the wall near the bar. Although the wine selection is nothing out of the ordinary, it does cover a reasonable international range, and the prices are hard to beat in this part of town. The Carriage House is ideal if you are looking for a relaxed, unpretentious venue with a 'local' ambience for a quick lunch or an after-work drink en route home.

Mint

182-186 St John Street, EC1
☎020 7253 8368
Mon-Fri: 11.30am - Midnight
Sat: 6pm - Midnight
27 @ £3.00 - £9.10
36 @ £13.80 - £185.00

Interesting international choice

A thirst-inducing walk up from the Tube, Mint's interior is as cool as its name. A symphony in various shades of brown greets new arrivals, with clever lighting adding new colour dimensions after dark. A long curved bar flanked by high stools is opposite a raised dining area, or sit back in one of the low-slung sofas to peruse the wine list. This covers an original range, served in ISO tasting glasses (very unusual), and the staff are happy to discuss choices. Mint is one of the few places in town to offer Flights, enabling curious quaffers to experiment with small tasting measures of wine. Choose from some of the house combinations, or make up one of your own from the list of wines by the glass.

www.mintbar.co.uk

Le Rendez-Vous du Café

121 Charterhouse Street, EC1
020 7336 8836
Mon-Fri: Noon - Midnight
11 @ £2.50 - £7.50
42 @ £9.00 - £48.00

French charm whatever the weather

In the corner of Charterhouse Street near the square, this bright and breezy bar-brasserie offers French chic at affordable prices. With stylish old-fashioned travel posters adorning the pale yellow walls, and French windows opening onto the pavement on warm days, you can feel transported across the Channel to a seaside resort. The marble-topped bar has glass shelves above it held in place by metal rods, from behind which the genial French host dispenses a Western European wine selection with the occasional New World guest. Slightly older vintages are available for those who prefer some age in the bottle. Live jazz features twice a month. Le Rendez-Vous has its regulars, but newcomers will enjoy making the discovery too.

Vic Naylor's Bar & Brasserie

38-42 St John Street, EC1
020 7608 2181
Mon-Fri: Noon - Midnight
Sat: 6pm - Midnight
9 @ £3.00 - £7.00
20 @ £12.00 - £35.00

Clerkenwell original still sets standards

Next to Vic Naylor's restaurant, friendly staff will redirect you if you pick the wrong front door. The bar area contains high-backed U-shaped booths, seating up to ten at a squash, and allowing intimate conversation without separating you from the action. Otherwise there are a pair of large rubber-topped tables at the back, where skylights let in light to counteract the den-like ambience nearer the door. The zinc and wood bar is long, with plenty of standing room if you haven't got a table. The bar wine list is selective; if you eat, you can ask for the full restaurant list. This opens up the choices considerably. Vic Naylor's has been here a long time, and has perfected its own inimitable brand of style and sophistication.

The Well

180 St John Street, EC1
020 7251 9363
Mon-Sat: 11am - 11pm
Sun: 11am - 10.30pm
12 @ £2.50 - £7.35
35 @ £9.95 - £350.00

Take the plunge

On the corner of St John and Compton Streets, The Well makes the most of its location with big picture windows revealing a clean blue, off-white and brick interior. The space is well-organised, with none of the tables so close together that you would feel uncomfortable having a private conversation. The wine list contains something for every pocket, and is drawn from all over the world. The most expensive wine is Château Pétrus 1992, not a famous year, but if you ordered a bottle of it you would obtain instant notoriety. Downstairs the mood changes completely, with the Aquarium Bar providing tranquil surroundings for a more laid-back experience. Watch the tropical fish as you relax on banquettes and pouffes scattered around, enjoy your glass of wine, and unwind.

Plus:

All Bar One
93a Charterhouse Street, EC1
020 7553 9391

Burgundy Ben's (Davy's)
102-108 Clerkenwell Road, EC1
020 7251 3783

Chez Gérard
84-86 Rosebery Avenue, EC1
020 7833 1515

The Sekforde Arms (Young's)
34 Sekforde Street, EC1
020 7253 3251

Auberge Bar Restaurant

56 Mark Lane, EC3
☎020 7480 6789
Mon-Fri: Noon - 11pm
17 @ £2.35 - £3.95
27 @ £9.95 - £49.95

Welcome shelter

We visited Auberge shortly after it first opened its doors on Mark Lane, and we are sure it will attract a large crowd. The massive subterranean bar and restaurant is approached through a welcoming entrance and down some stairs. A large crescent bar dominates to one side, while the other is full of tables for diners. Brightly lit and with vibrant modern décor, Auberge gives you a sense of bonhomie and an instant thirst! The wine list is simple and straightforward, with a range of weights and flavours to suit most palates.

Fenchurch Colony

14 New London Street, EC3
☎020 7481 0848
Mon-Fri: 11am - 11pm
14 @ £2.80 - £4.00
56 @ £10.90 - £98.00

Bold and brassy

Part of the mini-chain of Colony wine bars, this venue is split into two areas: the brasserie and bar, and the grill and bar. The latter is set up for more casual dining and quaffing, but both sides are modern, bright and busy with local clientele from nearby offices. As with the other Colony bars, this is a reliable venue for a good drop.

Ruskin's Bar and Restaurant

60 Mark Lane, EC3
☎020 7680 1234
Mon-Fri: 11am - 9pm
6 @ £3.00 - £3.80
51 @ £10.50 - £38.50

Crafted tranquility

This oasis lies in a basement on Mark Lane below the hubbub of day-to-day City life. Named after the 19th century writer and critic John Ruskin, the bar is situated in an historic building previously used for the storage of wines and spirits. Today, the stone interior is brightly coloured, pictures adorn the walls and the cool, pleasant atmosphere immediately conveys a sense of calm. Friendly staff are on hand to serve a client base drawn predominantly from local offices. The wine list contains a good range from the classic regions.

Plus:

City Flogger (Davy's) ⊖
Fen Court, 120 Fenchurch St, EC3
☎020 7623 3251

The Elephant (Young's) ⊖
119 Fenchurch Street, EC3
☎020 7623 89770

Jamies ⊖
Bankside House, 107-112 Leadenhall Street, EC3
☎020 7626 7226

Pitcher & Piano ⊖
The Arches, 9 Crutched Friars, EC3
☎020 7480 6818

Willy's Wine Bar (Young's) ⊖
107 Fenchurch Street, EC3
☎020 7480 7289

The Wine Lodge (Young's) ⊖
Sackville House, 145 Fenchurch Street, EC3
☎020 7626 0918

Fulham Broadway

The Front Room

562 King's Road, SW6
020 7736 3535
Mon-Sat: Noon - 11pm
Sun: Noon - 10.30pm
4 @ £2.75 - £3.25
17 @ £8.95 - £35.00

Home from home

One of the newer London bar chains, The Front Room recreates its version of the ideal living space of its target clientele, namely undomesticated 20- and 30-somethings. Imagine deep leather sofas, low tables and large televisions for watching major sporting events with your mates. The big advantage over home is that the drinks and food are handy but somebody else clears up. This Front Room benefits from afternoon sun, with French windows open at the merest hint of balmy temperatures, and pavement tables even in winter. The wine tends to get buried in the concept, but on closer inspection, you will find a respectable range of international choices at affordable prices.

www.thefrontroom.co.uk

Iguaçu

486 Fulham Road, SW6
020 7381 2372
Mon-Fri: 11am - 11.30pm
Sat & Sun: 10am - 11.30pm
6 @ £3.25 - £4.50 (250ml)
26 @ £10.95 - £45.95

Refreshingly different

In the heart of Fulham Broadway, this narrow-fronted bar-restaurant-café is intimate and friendly. There is a bar area as you go in, where smiling staff serve cocktails and wines from the European-flavoured list. Despite Brazilian inspiration, there is only one South American wine to choose. However on our visit this came with complimentary olives – delicious! The venue is full of tables and chairs, testament to its popularity as an eatery as well as being a fun place to have a drink. Iguaçu offers welcome variety in a world of bar chains and deserves to do well.

www.iguacu.co.uk

The Imperial

577 King's Road, SW6
020 7736 8549
Mon-Sat: Noon - 11pm
Sun: 12.30pm - 10.30pm
8 @ £2.30 - £3.20
13 @ £10.50 - £33.00

Popular pub

Bright blue on a corner among the glossy black fronts of King's Road antiques emporia, the Imperial certainly stands out. Painted devilish red inside in keeping with the pub's pitchfork symbol, there are some sofas and various tables but also masses of standing room. While the Imperial caters mainly for a young, big screen sports-watching, beer- and cocktail-drinking crowd, it also has its refined side. Board games are available and the daily menu looks to be good value. The wine selection is somewhat limited, but what there is has a New World focus, and provides a decent alternative for those who prefer grape to grain.

Joe's Brasserie

130 Wandsworth Bridge Road, SW6
020 7731 7835
Mon-Sun: Noon - 11pm
None listed
36 @ £5.00 - £30.00

No need to pine for wine

Set among the pine shops of the Chelsea/Fulham border, Joe's Brasserie has an easy charm which sits well with the traders who spend their days making furniture on the wide pavements. In summer an outdoor seating area brings customers closer to the steady flow of passersby, while a chequer-floored salon inside offers shelter if the weather should suddenly change. The style is continental, with a bar area separated from the dining section by a partition down the centre of the main room. Wines are very reasonable (Joe's has recently been acquired by the Brinkley's group), covering a standard international range which will appeal to everyone. A great place to come for a lazy lunch, a few drinks, and to watch the world stroll by.

The Pelican

22 Waterford Road, SW6
☎020 7736 1023
Mon-Sun: Noon - 11pm
11 @ £2.50 - £4.40
24 @ £8.95 - £86.50

Posh local

For that is effectively what the Pelican is. On the corner of Moore Park and Waterford Roads, not far from the Tube, this is a lively venue frequented both by residents and by those parachuting into Fulham in search of fun. Towards the end of the week it heaves with youth and vitality, so isn't really the place for a quiet drink; however during the day it takes on a more peaceful guise. Potted plants and warm terracotta-coloured walls give it a touch more character than other pub-bars in its league. The wines cater for all tastes in both range and price, demonstrating that the Pelican aspires to be more than just a beer barn.

Plus:

All Bar One
587-591 Fulham Road, SW6
☎020 7471 0611

Scandie's

4 Kynance Place, SW7
☎020 7589 3659
Mon-Fri: 5pm - 11pm
Sat: 6pm - 11pm; Sun: 6pm - 10.30pm
13 @ £2.75 - £5.95
33 @ £10.95 - £34.95

Perfect for dinner

This intimate little bar and restaurant is about half-way up Gloucester Road between the Tube and Kensington Gardens. Clever use of mirrors makes the room look bigger than it really is, with cosy tables and chairs and red-and-cream paintwork adding to the bistro style. Potted geraniums draw the eye in summer. As well as a decent selection of French wines, there are Old and New World offerings plus specials and promotions. Unless you were a local resident you might not venture this far into the mansion blocks of Kensington just to drink wine, but if you were to combine it with dinner, Scandie's provides an unpretentious venue in which to enjoy a night out.

Plus:

All Bar One
152 Gloucester Road, SW7
☎020 7244 5861

Flute's Wine Bar & Brasserie

61 Goodge Street, W1
☎020 7637 0177
Mon-Fri: 11.30am - 11.30pm
20 @ £2.50 - £5.50
55 @ £9.50 - £32.95

Cheery charm

Thank goodness places like Flute's still thrive in Central London, where rent and the influence of the ubiquitous bar chains threaten anything with an individual streak. This bar fills a long narrow space down metal stairs a couple of blocks along Goodge Street. It's painted yellow and dark red, with an impressive array of autographed black-and-white photos of film stars on the walls, and wooden shipping boxes pinned up to remind you that this is a bona fide wine bar. The list presents a selection dominated by French wines, and the international offerings are well-chosen. Staff are welcoming, and the clientele is a mixed bag drawn from local media enterprises and those who are already familiar with Flute's excellent value and service.

The Mortimer

40 Berners Street, W1
☎020 7436 0451
Mon-Sat: Noon - 11pm
13 @ £2.50 - £5.00
30 @ £9.90 - £39.90

Spot and be spotted

On the corner with Mortimer Street, hence the name, this is a big open bar which hides nothing away. Huge picture windows on two sides allow observation in and out, and the canteen grill is a continuation of the long zinc-clad bar. Green is the theme, offering calm and tranquillity in London's medialand. Choose a soft banquette or a more conventional table and chair arrangement at which to enjoy something from the wine selection. The list has a lot of French choices and is strong on Australian wines too, plus the inevitable international tokens. Everything is written up on blackboard menus above the bar, handy when the place gets packed later in the day.

Plus:

Jamies

74 Charlotte Street, W1
☎020 7636 7556

The One Tun (Young's)

58-60 Goodge Street, W1
☎020 7209 4105

L'Artiste Musclé

1 Shepherd Market, Mayfair, W1
020 7493 6150
Mon-Sat: Noon - Midnight
Sun: Noon - 11.30pm
7 @ £2.60 - £3.00
32 @ £9.90 - £35.00

Oh là là!

The original owner of this tiny bar at the end of White Horse Street was a wrestling silversmith, hence the name. Now the French influence remains, with each of the two intimate rooms adorned with old enamelled advertising or street signs and evocative posters. The wine list is exclusively French, with all main regions represented. Being away from the traffic fumes of nearby Piccadilly and Hyde Park Corner in pretty Shepherd Market, the bar is tremendously popular. If you are here at lunch or supper time it's best to be eating, or you risk having nowhere to sit and enjoy the lively atmosphere of this little gem.

Dover Street Restaurant & Bar

8-10 Dover Street, W1
020 7491 7509
Mon-Fri: Noon - 3pm/5.30pm - 3am
Sat: 6pm - 3am
7 @ £3.75 - £6.25
60 @ £12.95 - £125.00

Jazz and wine make you feel fine

If jazz is your thing but you also appreciate refined elegance, head for Mayfair and this series of smartly turned-out basement rooms. For twenty-two years Dover Street has promoted live music as much as its French/Mediterranean cuisine and accompanying wines, establishing a healthy reputation among the capital's jazz lovers. Although the emphasis is on French wines to match the cooking, you will find a broad range of international choices as well. On Fridays and Saturdays the place is so popular that there is only room for diners, and you need to be aware of cover charges for the music after certain points in the evening.

Fino's Wine Bar & Restaurant

123 Mount Street, W1
020 7491 1640
Mon-Fri: 11.30am - 11pm
Sat: 6pm - 11pm
10 @ £1.90 - £5.20 (125ml)
64 @ £9.50 - £124.50

Italian wines a feature

Not far from Berkeley Square, Fino's is a real find in the heart of Mayfair. Highly polished brass door fittings are the only exterior concession to its location, tucked in next to a mansion block. Go straight down narrow stairs to a labyrinthine basement, with a long wooden bar as the link between various alcoves and rooms. There's masses of seating and standing room, plenty of dark wood and unique old-fashioned style in which to sample something from the wine list. This emphasises Italy and France in equal measure, with other Western European wines making up the numbers. The lunchtime crowd is gents in suits talking politics and banking, making the most of Fino's value-for-money service.

Just Oriental

19 King Street, SW1
020 7930 9292
Mon-Sat: Noon - 11pm
12 @ £3.50 - £7.50
29 @ £12.50 - £48.00

East-West value for money

On the corner of St James's Street, Just Oriental bar-brasserie fills the basement of an old bank, and can be approached from King Street, or from its sister establishment directly above. An expansive bar area contains a dining section, as well as booths and comfortable seating for those who just want to enjoy wine or cocktails. Subtle lighting and the occasional piece of oriental furniture enhance the ambience without being ostentatious. The owner has a vineyard in Sussex, and one of his wines is on the internationally-inspired list. For those who need even more choice, the restaurant list can be obtained from upstairs. Delicious fusion food completes the picture, providing excellent value in this part of the capital.

Plus:

Balls Brothers
20 St James's Street, SW1
☎020 7321 0882

Chez Gérard
31 Dover Street, W1
☎020 7499 8171

Davy's at St James's
Crown Passage, Pall Mall, SW1
☎020 7839 8831

The Guinea (Young's)
30 Bruton Place, Berkeley Square, SW1
☎020 7409 1728

Pitcher & Piano
1 Dover Street, W1
☎020 7495 8704

Bar 38
4 Queen Caroline Street, W6
☎020 8748 3951
Mon-Sat: 11am - 11pm
Sun: 3pm - 10.30pm
19 @ £2.60 - £5.35
19 @ £9.95 - £85.00

Broadway bonus

Opposite the Hammersmith Broadway development, Bar 38 provides a lively venue for its varied clientele, and is ideally located between the main shopping area and the Apollo theatre. The bar has huge picture windows and standard-issue wooden furniture and floors, with the occasional interesting object on the walls or suspended from the ceiling to challenge the more familiar design elements. Two floors linked by a sweeping curved staircase provide ample room for customers to relax and enjoy the food and drink on offer. Wines are at the quaffing end of the spectrum, covering an international range. Consequently there are no surprises in store, but the number available by the glass ensures plenty of choice if you are just after some quick vinous refreshment.

Hammersmith

Martin's Wine Bar

170-172 Hammersmith Road, W6
☎020 8741 7843
Mon-Fri: Noon - 11pm
10 @ £2.50 - £2.75
20 @ £8.50 - £27.50

Wine with a sense of humour

Over the years Martin's has changed from being a typical '80s wine bar into more of an all-purpose local for residents and office workers. The bar itself is a den downstairs, reached by walking past some curious looks from those in the street-level food serving area. Wines on offer change at the whim of the owner, and in accordance with the wishes of regulars. On our visit, they were in an Italian phase; before that it was everything Australian. Said wines are presented on a conference message board behind the bar, often in pun form. Anyone for Peanut Grigio? Sincerre? Mus G'Day? If you want friendly banter and are prepared to take your wine a little less seriously than usual, give Martin's a try.

Plus:

Brook Green (Young's)
170 Shepherd's Bush Road, W6
☎020 7603 2516

Hammersmith Ram (Young's)
81 King Street, W6
☎020 8748 4511

Highgate

Idaho

13 North Hill, N6
☎020 8341 6633
Mon-Sat: 12.30pm - 11pm
Sun: 12.30pm - 10pm
13 @ £3.00 - £7.00
48 @ £12.00 - £135.00

Northern star

Emerging from the Tube, the first thing that hits you is the leafiness of this part of London, followed closely by its height above the city. To find the venue you will be able to enjoy the greenery further, as it's a 5-10 minute stroll through the Park Walk shortcut from Southwood Lane to North Hill. Idaho blends into its surroundings, looking more like one of the neighbouring residential mansions than the coolly elegant bar-restaurant that it is. This is modern drinking and dining at its best, with an imaginative international wine list (which includes quality Central European wines, and Priorato, the rising star from Spain). Idaho dares to be different and Highgate reaps the benefit.

Plus:

All Bar One
1-3 Hampstead Lane, N6
☎020 8342 7861

The Abingdon

54 Abingdon Road, W8
020 7937 3339
Mon-Sat: 12.30pm - 11pm
Sun: 12.30pm - 10.30pm
13 @ £3.00 - £6.50
44 @ £10.75 - £48.50

All in the best possible taste

Set on a leafy corner about 100m off Kensington High Street, this gastropub is a popular local haunt attracting customers of all ages. The bar itself is centrally placed between two main areas. Bar stools, chintzy sofas which could grace any living room in the neighbourhood, and high-legged tables at which to perch for drinking or relaxed eating fill the first room; a more formal style reigns on the dining side of an internal window partition. The Abingdon is fêted for its food, and the wine list is also impressive, with an interesting range of grape varieties included in the international selection. Refined yet relaxed style is the watchword here, as befits the locale.

L'Anis Bar & Restaurant

1 Kensington High Street, W8
020 7795 6533
Mon-Fri: Noon - Midnight
Sat: 6pm - Midnight
12 @ £3.50 - £7.00
131 @ £13.50 - £510.00

Sophisticated selection and space

Opposite the south-western corner of Kensington Gardens, L'Anis is housed inside an ornate mid-Victorian room, with elaborate drapes at high windows, panelled wooden walls, and sculpted door frames. Yet the bar, on a raised platform by the door, is a triumph of modern styling. Leather chairs, subtle chrome and subdued lighting contribute to chic elegance, as does a glass sculpture on one end of the bar. L' Anis is intending to add another fifty bottles to its already exceptional wine list before the end of 2001. Half of it is French, including several vintages and all the traditional regions; the remainder comprises some quality offerings from the rest of the world. The management welcomes casual drinkers as well as those staying on to dine, so treat yourself!

Benedict's Restaurant & Wine Bar

106 Kensington High Street, W8
020 7937 7580
Mon-Fri: Noon - 3pm/5pm - 10.30pm
Sat: Noon - 10.30pm; Sun: 1pm - 8pm
6 @ £2.35 - £5.55
28 @ £8.99 - £29.99

Age of chivalry not yet dead

Up steep stairs opposite the Tube, Benedict's appears to be a throwback to past times, with heavy wooden tables and chairs, ageing carpet, and a tiny bar-servery jammed in by the door. A monastic theme is established by prints of friars in varying states of inebriation, with wine acknowledged by the stencilled ends of wooden bottle-shipping boxes. But give yourself a moment to adjust, and you will find that Benedict's does its job very well: moderate in every respect, from affordable wines to well-priced hearty food not readily available on the High Street below. If you are lucky enough to get a table by the window it's ideal for surveying the scene outside, content in the knowledge that you are enjoying old-fashioned manners and excellent value.

High Street Kensington

Goolie's Bar & Restaurant

21 Abingdon Road, W8
☎020 7938 1122
Mon-Sat: Noon - 11pm
Sun: Noon - 10.30pm
15 @ £2.75 - £7.50
44 @ £10.95 - £125.00

Familiar formula

Goolie's is the kind of bar you can find all over London: a cut above the ubiquitous chains, but not quite brave enough to be truly original. For all that, it provides all the ingredients in a palatable package. Pale wood, banquettes, unusual wrought-iron fittings, and a chunky bar top create a modern feel, with light flooding in to the front section of the bar through plate glass windows. For a more intimate experience, the dining mezzanine at the back is suitably subdued. The wine list is orientated towards the New World, although room is found for some Old World representatives. Modern British cuisine completes the equation. It all adds up to a pleasant place to come for a quiet drink, but expect no surprises.

Plus:

The Brittania (Young's)

1 Allen Street, W8
☎020 7937 6905

Holborn

Bank Aldwych

1 Kingsway, WC2
☎020 7379 9797
Mon-Fri: 7.30am - 11.30pm
Sat: 11.30am - 11.30pm
Sun: 11.30am - 10pm
14 @ £3.40 - £7.75
67 @ £12.90 - £189.00

Round the bend

At the top of the Aldwych curve behind the BBC World Service at Bush House, Bank is home to an elongated marble-topped U-shape, otherwise known as the bar. Beyond this is the restaurant per se, but drinkers can gather at the front of the space to enjoy one of the many wines or cocktails available. Here there are both bar stools and grouped tables and chairs overlooking the street, where customers can relax in sophisticated surroundings. The international wine list contains many pleasures, and for those with money to burn there is a small selection of cellar wines from which to choose that special vintage. Forget the overdraft and enjoy the good things in life!
www.bankrestaurants.com

Cort's Holborn Bar & Restaurant

78 High Holborn, WC1
☎020 7242 4292
Mon-Fri: 11.30am - 11pm
10 @ £2.90 - £6.00
35 @ £9.50 - £125.00

Modern take on established favourite

This offshoot of the Cort's bar in Chancery Lane is the young, trendy kid brother to the more serious older sibling. Royal blue and orange colour complements the pale wood so beloved of modern designers, but the atmosphere is far from being intimidatingly cool. Conversely, staff are super-friendly and helpful, making this an ideal place for everything from a business lunch to a fun night out with friends to a party in one of the separate function rooms. A huge picture window overlooks the traffic on High Holborn, but inside all is calm. Wines cover an excellent selection of international choices. By the glass it's not the cheapest in town, but the bottles represent decent value for money.

Parker's Wine Bar & Restaurant

109 Kingsway, WC2
☎020 7242 5426
Mon-Fri: Noon - 3pm
None listed
29 @ £9.95 - £39.00

Lunchtime special

Look for Parker Street off Kingsway and you will see this rather traditional wine bar tucked into a corner. Although only open at lunchtime or for private functions, it makes a pleasant change from the numerous bar chains and restaurants out in Kingsway proper. There is a bar area at the front, with wicker chairs, tables and pot-plants to brighten the interior. Wines are international, with mid-'90s vintages available for some, and all at reasonable prices. The food also looks appealing, with several fish dishes on a menu which includes omelettes and hearty sandwiches. Ideal if you fancy sharing a bottle with a friend.

Harley's Café Bar

266-267 High Holborn, WC1
☎020 7242 4350
Mon-Fri: 11am - 11pm
8 @ £2.75 - £4.95
18 @ £9.75 - £79.95

Mature modern bar

Harley's contains elements of all the London bar chains without actually being one itself: strong modern paint colours, blond wood, slate floor. In other words, it doesn't announce itself as anything out of the ordinary. The atmosphere is rather subdued, suggesting that the clientele is slightly older than the usual 20-something bar chain crowd. In summer, French windows open out onto the wide pavement in front of the bar. The wine list is international, including a Greek white which is about the only surprise you'll find in here. For reliable wines, albeit run-of-the-mill, Harley's is a safe option.

Plus:

All Bar One

58 Kingsway, WC2
☎020 7269 5171

Bung Hole (Davy's)

57 High Holborn, WC1
☎020 7831 8365

The Fine Line

77 Kingsway, WC2
☎020 7405 5004

Jamies

50-54 Kingsway, WC2
☎020 7405 9749

Pitcher & Piano

42 Kingsway, WC2
☎020 7404 8510

Truckles of Pied Bull Yard (Davy's)

Pied Bull Yard, Off Bury Place, WC1
☎020 7404 5338

Holland Park

Julie's Bar

137 Portland Road, W11
020 7727 7985
Mon-Sat: 9am - 11pm
Sun: 10am - 10.30pm
9 @ £2.95 - £5.95
41 @ £11.95 - £55.00

Absolutely bazaar

Something of an institution in this part of town, Julie's combines a unique decorative style with a reputation for good cooking and fine wines. The bar itself is a cosy corner at the front of a maze of nooks and crannies which spread back into an intimate restaurant; in summer, a delightful terrace in the pedestrian plaza outside is an attractive proposition. Oriental screens and artefacts make the interior seem more like a wealthy hippy's paean to the sub-continent, but there is no doubt that the food and drink owe more to the current zeitgeist. Wines, which include several mid-'90s vintages (not that common), are international with French bottles leading the way. Reliable producers from elsewhere also feature. Thoroughly civilised and definitely unique.

Kentish Town

The Bull & Last

168 Highgate Road, NW5
020 7267 3641
Mon-Fri: 11am - 11pm
Sun: 11am - 10.30pm
10 @ £2.50 - £3.75
24 @ £10.00 - £19.50

Bellissimo!

On the corner of Woodsome Street some distance from the Tube, you may prefer to hop onto a bus to reach this sunny gastropub more quickly. However you get here, you will find a friendly reception and comfortable surroundings. The main room contains an eclectic collection of oak and leather furniture and a standard lamp, with the walls hung with changing art exhibitions. You can even make a purchase, should the mood take you. Upstairs there's a dining room, and the menu has an Italian influence. This theme follows on the wine list, the majority of choices being from Italy, with the New World also represented. Right near Hampstead Heath, this makes a great start or finish point for a weekend ramble.

The Vine

86 Highgate Road, NW5
020 7209 0038
Mon-Sat: Noon - Midnight
Sun: Noon - 11.30pm
4 @ £2.75 - £3.50
24 @ £9.95 - £45.95

Rich pickings

Having undergone the gastropub treatment, The Vine has established a solid reputation as purveyor of fine cuisine and beverages to the cognoscenti of NW5. The forecourt with picnic tables next to the street shrieks standard pub, but inside is another story altogether. There are several spaces for drinking or dining and another outdoor area at the rear, none of these too far from a central copper-clad bar. It's busy with satisfied customers taking advantage of the fare, which includes an extensive European-with-a-twist menu and a carefully-chosen international wine selection. Don't let the lack of by-the-glass choices defeat you; this is the kind of place to linger while sharing a bottle with friends.

Smithy's Wine Bar & Restaurant

Leeke Street, WC1
☎020 7278 5949
Mon-Fri: 11am - 11pm
All available from £2.30
Tons from £9.00

One out of the bag

More or less on the corner of Leeke and Wicklow Streets, Smithy's is a law unto itself in both style and presentation. Warm, relaxed and original, the interior reflects the forge alluded to in the name, with cobbled floors and high industrial girders and skylights above. The grill in the back corner blazes as the blacksmith's fire must once have done, and it's always heaving with hungry diners. Wines are chalked on blackboards all around the walls, with undoubtedly the finest regional coverage available in London. Nowhere else have we seen Israeli, Mexican, Lebanese, Swiss and English wines in the same location. For the less adventurous, more traditional vinous fare is offered, with special purchase wines to be found in amongst the literally hundreds of choices. Seeing is believing!

A Bar 2 Far

1-6 Market Place, The Griffin Centre, KT1
☎020 8546 5226
Mon-Sat: 11am - 11pm
Sun: Noon - 10.30pm
12 @ £2.75 - £6.00
14 @ £10.50 - £27.50

Beyond the fringe

First find the square, then keep your eyes open for the alley which leads towards the river, and to A Bar 2 Far. The whole Charter Quay area is being redeveloped, and this particular bar has got in first in a former hotel. Split into two rooms, downstairs has a light and breezy Mediterranean café feel, while the second space in an old ballroom upstairs is a more sophisticated lounge and dancing area. Tables outdoors complete the picture. Wines are the standard international selection, but there are a couple of surprises lurking to make life interesting. Kingston is not currently blessed with many choices for drinking wine, so it's worth tracking this place down.
www.abar2far.com

Plus:

Bishop Out of Residence (Young's)

2 Bishop's Hall, Off Thames Street, KT1
☎020 8546 4965

Isola

145 Knightsbridge, SW1
☎020 7838 1044
Mon-Sat: 5pm - Midnight
26 @ £3.90 - £35.00
239 @ £14.50 - £490.00

Classic Italian job

Around the corner from the main shopping zone of Knightsbridge, Isola benefits from its slight distance from the madding crowd. There are no obvious signs to announce its presence; instead you need to keep a lookout for big plate glass windows and a "Push to Open" button which operates the sliding entry door. Inside lies the epitome of top-flight Italian design, stylish yet practical, but the wines are the real star here. Exclusively Italian, the list covers every region, and some wines are offered in multiple vintages. The full restaurant wine list is available on request if the one in the bar is not enough to set your tastebuds tingling. For lovers of Italian wine, a visit to Isola is essential.

Le Métro

28 Basil Street, SW3
☎020 7591 1213
Mon-Sat: 7.30am - 11pm
25 @ £2.85 - £7.25
28 @ £10.95 - £52.00

Sophistication at affordable prices

A waist-height sign on a small railing is all that exists to tell you where to find Le Métro. It's underneath L'Hôtel on the right side of Basil Street, near the back entrances to Harrods. Down some metal stairs is a bijou basement, whose limited space is enhanced with judicious use of colour and mirrors. From the comfort of chintzy soft furnishings or more formal tables and chairs you can order wine from a list which favours France but is not exclusive. If Knightsbridge shop prices have knocked you out, Le Métro is the place to come for a restorative drink, knowing that you will find value for money despite the location.

Swag & Tails

10-11 Fairholt Street, SW7
☎020 7584 6926
Mon-Fri: 11am - 11pm
10 @ £2.95 - £5.00
34 @ £10.95 - £150.00

Half the fun is getting there!

Not the easiest place to find, well-hidden in pretty mews streets behind the busy Brompton Road, Swag & Tails rewards those who persevere. One of London's original gastropubs, it has a reputation for good food and well-chosen wines. These are listed by varietal and include internationally-renowned names such as New Zealand's Cloudy Bay and Jaboulet from the Rhône. The bar is decked out in pale wood and navy blue, with drapes at the windows and a dried flower frieze attached to the cornice. Wine artefacts and interesting prints give focal points should conversation flag. To the rear is a conservatory and further dining area. Here for twelve years, Swag & Tails has a loyal following, from old stagers to local business people and residents, but new faces are always welcome.

Leicester Square

Le Beaujolais

25 Litchfield Street, WC2
☎020 7836 2955
Mon-Fri: Noon - 11pm
Sat: 5pm -11pm
13 @ £2.60 - £6.00
56 @ £9.80 - £34.50

Best-kept secret in town

If you are dedicated to the product of the hills and valleys between Mâcon and Lyon, look no further than Le Beaujolais. Here you will find a happy band of like-minded devotees, somewhat proprietorial about their bastion of Beaujolais, but at the same time keen to welcome true believers. All ten Beaujolais Crus are represented on the entirely French list, and if you become a familiar face in here the staff will recommend new treats that come in. These people really care about wine and want to share their knowledge and appreciation with other connoisseurs. Le Beaujolais gets absolutely packed and often has to turn people away. But pick your moment, and once you have a foot in the door it will prove hard to leave.

Cork & Bottle Wine Bar

44-46 Cranbourn Street, WC2
☎020 7734 7807
Mon-Sat: 11am - Midnight
Sun: Noon - 10.30pm
24 @ £3.00 - £6.00
182 @ £11.50 - £235.00

Fair dinkum!

Don't confuse the Cork & Bottle with the sex shop or the ticket agency on either side of it! Instead descend past wine posters and old bottles to reach the reassuringly well-lit bar and dining area. Owner Don Hewitson fancies himself as a High Priest of Wine, and with good reason. Both his wine list (Australasia a speciality) and his regular newsletters describe his annual struggle on behalf of vinophiles to discover the best from Europe and the New World. There's something here for every taste and budget. Despite the address, it's not a tourist trap, but should you venture into this underworld, it may be difficult to escape.

www.donhewitsonlondonwinebars.co.uk

Corney & Barrow

116 St Martin's Lane, WC2
☎020 7655 9800
Mon-Wed: Noon - Midnight
Thu-Sat: Noon - 2am
44 @ £2.95 - £9.90
80 @ £11.25 - £125.00

Flagship of well-known chain

Imposingly located in an old bank opposite the National Portrait Gallery at the foot of Charing Cross Road, the West End branch of the C&B chain sets out the stall for its City counterparts to emulate. The shell of the building has been modernised with plenty of glass and steel, pale flagstones on the floors, and three storeys of drinking and dining space. The venue licence is attributable to a members' policy, so if you arrive late in the evening you will be asked to pay a cover charge. The rest of the time however, you can enjoy a glass or a bottle from the excellent selection which is presented in a comprehensively detailed list. Champagne takes pride of place here in a separate bar which opens at 6pm.

Leicester Square

The French House

49 Dean Street, Soho, W1
020 7437 2799
Mon-Sat: Noon - 11pm
Sun: Noon - 10.30pm
19 @ £2.20 - £5.50 (125ml)
19 @ £11.00 - £40.50

Flying the flag for France

Look out for the tricolours (French and Union) hanging down from the French House at the southern end of Dean Street, and you will have spotted one of the friendliest and least pretentious of Soho's many watering holes. "The French", as it is known locally, has an illustrious past which can be read in a book borrowed from behind the bar, but it's unlikely that you will read in peace because one of the fascinating characters here will want to gather you into conversation before long. The walls are lined with photos, cartoons and press cuttings of glory days gone by, but sitting here enjoying a pleasant drop of French wine (or a glass of Rioja, the only outsider on the list), you get the feeling that you are part of history in the making.

Garrick Wine Bar & Restaurant

10-12 Garrick Street, WC2
020 7240 7649
Mon-Wed: Noon - 11pm
Thu-Sat: Noon - Midnight
11 @ £2.30 - £4.90 (125ml)
22 @ £9.95 - £37.70

Cosy quaffing

In the heart of Theatreland, the Garrick is a popular pre-show destination, as well as attracting office workers during the day. Squeezed into a ground floor room from which a spiral staircase descends into a candlelit cavern below, it's hard to think where they could put any more tables. Even the bar is only just big enough for setting up a couple of glasses and a bottle. The relatively dark interior gives the place an air of mystery, and intimate alcoves downstairs are a real bonus for those with a romantic bent. French wines fill the list, with some international choices also available, plus several wines of the week. If you're off to see "Les Misérables", this Gallic interpretation of theatrical tradition will put you in just the right mood.

Kettner's Champagne Bar

29 Romilly Street, Soho, W1
020 7734 6112
Mon-Sun: 11am - Midnight
1 @ £6.25
83 @ £26.50 - £170.00

How many?

Lovers of the fizzy stuff should not go past Kettner's, home to no less than thirty-two marques of Champagne, with no still wines listed. Enjoy the bubbles in the civilised surroundings of a ground floor bar, divided into two sections. One of these resembles a hotel lounge, with armchairs and rugs scattered around. To the rear, a gallery-like space opens out with more modern furnishings and abstract art on the walls. As far as we are aware, nowhere else in London offers such an extensive Champagne selection, with seventeen rosé wines listed, and a fair share of half-bottles, magnums and larger biblical measures also available. Prices are generally more reasonable than at other Champagne-orientated locations too.

Signor Zilli Bar

40 Dean Street, Soho, W1
☎020 7734 1853
Mon-Sat: Noon - Midnight
12 @ £3.00 - £5.50
31 @ £10.50 - £48.00

Smooth operator

Halfway along Dean Street, Signor Zilli is adjacent to its brother-restaurant of the same name, and both have an Italian emphasis in food and wines. Signor Zilli is the epitome of a contemporary continental café, all blond wood and stylish curved bar, good-looking staff efficiently serving youthful designer-clad clientele or Soho media types, either indoors or at the pavement tables outside. Although the room is relatively small, there is ample space between tables, so intimate conversation is just as feasible as group bantering. The wine list is two-thirds Italian in origin, with the remainder made up of New World or French bottles. Although one of the plethora of style-conscious bars in Soho, Signor Zilli is still not so overwhelmed by its own cool that you couldn't drop in here for a relaxed drink or two.

La Tartine

14 Garrick Street, WC2
☎020 7379 1531
Mon-Fri: Noon - 11pm
4 @ £2.60 - £4.70
26 @ £10.00 - £47.00

Allez France!

La Tartine is reached through the front door of L'Estaminet restaurant, from where you take the stairs into the basement bar. En route, French signs and rugby memorabilia show you the way. Once inside, the décor is standard Central London wine bar and clearly this one is very popular. "Best wine bar in Covent Garden" announced one customer in between mouthfuls of steak-frites and sips of red. Wines here are exclusively French, to be enjoyed at the bar on a high stool or at one of the banquettes around the edge of the room. For rugby fans, the framed posters, programmes and tickets are a fascinating record of some classic matches – providing a great excuse to drop in here for a glass or two.

Plus:

All Bar One
84 Cambridge Circus, WC2
☎020 7379 8311

All Bar One
36-38 Dean Street, W1
☎020 7479 7921

All Bar One
48 Leicester Square, WC2
☎020 7747 9921

Café Med
22-25 Dean Street, W1
☎020 7287 9007

Pitcher & Piano
69-70 Dean Street, W1
☎020 7434 3585

The Bolt Hole

8a Artillery Passage, E1
020 7247 5056
Mon-Fri: 11am - 9pm
10 @ £2.90 - £6.00
22 @ £10.80 - £50.00

By name and by nature!

An appropriate name for a cosy, modern, trendy bar tucked away in a tiny passage just away from the hurly burly of Bishopsgate and Liverpool Street station. The Bolt Hole is both friendly and relaxed, but has the potential to become the Black Hole if too many of the local office population descend on it after working hours. Not the first choice in this area for the committed wine quaffer, but nevertheless a safe option for a good quality glass of wine.

Chapters Wine Bar & Restaurant

166-170 Bishopsgate, EC2
020 7247 8992
Mon-Wed: 11am - 9pm
Thu & Fri: 11am - 10pm
12 @ £2.70 - £3.70
69 @ £10.50 - £130.00

Plus ça change...

A rather glamorous long staircase leads down to a marbled and chromed bar-dining room. Curves and etched glass complete the scene, with subtle lighting adding to the ambience. This is a standard City wine bar, with a range of bar snacks and meals, and a full restaurant menu. Likewise, the wine list covers the expected bases, with French and Italian vintages a speciality, and featured wines which change frequently. In many respects Chapters doesn't differ greatly from some of the better-known City wine bar chains, but it's reassuring to know that you can enjoy something familiar in an alternative venue. **www.mithrasbars.co.uk**.

Brodie's

16 Eldon Street, EC2
020 7256 7780
Mon-Fri: 11am - 11pm
16 @ £2.90 - £4.70
44 @ £11.20 - £55.20

Bonus in the basement

One of four Brodie's establishments in the City, this outlet is opposite the main entrance to the Broadgate development. Take the impressive slate staircase, or the lift, down to a basement bar which spreads out underground, and is surprisingly bright for a subterranean venue. There are prints of London event and transport posters from a bygone era, and plenty of brass around the long curved bar to boost the light quotient. The reasonably extensive wine list contains Old and New World standards, with French bottles in the majority. All wines are competitively priced, and with a decent selection of bar meals or the restaurant menu to tempt you further, Brodie's has something for everyone.

Cozy's Wine Bar & Restaurant

11 Sun Street, EC2
020 7247 9445
Mon & Tue: 11am - 10pm
Wed-Fri: 11am - Midnight
5 @ £3.00 - £3.75
36 @ £9.95 - £150.00

Curious combination

Cozy's looks quite promising from the outside, with corks piled up in the window indicating that there are good times to be had here. Once inside, framed photos of movie icons look down on dining tables, before you reach a bar at the back of the room. Here the manager holds forth, and Cozy's feels more like a local or a members' club to a first-time visitor. This can be off-putting, which is a shame because the wine list is decent enough. Mainly French, with some international class, prices tend to reflect the location near all those City salaries (and bonuses). Seven wines of the month add interest as well.

Earl's Restaurant & Wine Bar

21-25 Earl Street, EC2
☎020 7375 0075
Mon-Fri: 11.45am - 2.30pm
5 @ £3.25 - £4.50
87 @ £12.00 - £245.00

Modern midday magic

Open only at lunchtimes, Earl's is the archetypal modern City wine establishment. Walk past the street-level restaurant down stairs to a spacious basement, where a small bar area is supplemented by plentiful seating. The ambience is informal but smart, tastfeul prints hang on the walls and there are nibbles on the bar counter. In fact, most customers come here to enjoy tasty Italian cuisine and a good bottle of wine, hence a lack of wines by the glass. However the bar and restaurant lists more than make up for this, with a big choice of quality French and Italian vintages as well as international standards.

Eaton's at the Broadgate

33 Broadgate Circle, EC2
☎020 7628 1592
Mon-Fri: 11am - 11pm
12 @ £2.90 - £4.95
45 @ £11.00 - £120.00

Liquid assets

The Broadgate development is home to many things, one of which is a winter ice rink. In the circular promenade around the rink's base lies Eaton's, a large comfortable bar which provides a warm welcome at any time of year. Wood predominates, with a collection of prints of monks in different states of inebriation on the walls (although the staff are not sure why this theme has emerged). Wine bottles stacked behind the bar and in an old-fashioned wine store along a side wall remind customers of one of the best reasons to come to Eaton's: an international list which concentrates on France, and represents value for money. As an alternative to the plethora of local bar chains, Eaton's makes a refreshing change.

Fishmarket Champagne Bar

Great Eastern Hotel, Bishopsgate, EC2
☎020 7618 7200
Mon-Fri: 11.30am - 11pm
Sat: 6pm - 11pm
14 @ £3.50 - £9.85
79 @ £12.95 - £574.00

Fizz bang for afishionados!

With thirty-six sparkling wines, this opulent bar is a magnet for lovers of bubbles. In the Great Eastern Hotel beside Liverpool Street Station, it makes the most of its ground floor location. Dark chocolate brown paint covers the original panelling, and a marble-topped elongated "O" in the centre of the space serves as the bar. The fish theme is developed in dark pastel crayon drawings framed on the walls. An impressive selection of seafood includes oysters and caviar to accompany the many wines. With the emphasis on things aquatic, red wines are scarce (only nine listed), but don't let this put you off. Friendly, efficient service enhances the experience: you will pay more than elsewhere, but will be well looked after.
www.fish-market.co.uk

Futures Café-Bar

2 Exchange Square, EC2
☎020 7638 6341
Mon-Fri: 7am - 10pm
9 @ £2.75 - £5.10
29 @ £9.95 - £54.95

Bright oasis in the urban desert

If you've never been into the Broadgate development which looms behind Liverpool Street station, it's worth a diversion. Look out for tall rectangular metal signposts on the pavement in Bishopsgate to find Exchange Square, where Futures sits near the buxom Broadgate Venus (it's a statue). The Mediterranean vibe inside this glass-sided space makes a welcome contrast to the high-rise austerity outside, and in any weather it's a great spot for looking out at whatever might be happening in the square. The wines on offer represent a respectable international range, with user-friendly prices. The food menu changes daily and you can even email through your order to **www1e.btwebworld.com/futures1/** (yes, it looks like an odd address but it definitely works!).

Lime

1 Curtain Road, EC2
020 7247 2225
Mon-Wed: 11am - 11.30pm
Thu & Fri: 11am - 1am
9 @ £3.95 - £8.60 (250ml)
30 @ £11.70 - £110.00

Dare to be different

Just beyond Broadgate to the north of Liverpool Street station, Lime lives up to its name with bright green paintwork and a zesty atmosphere which appeals to City types as well as Shoreditch movers and shakers. An easy stroll from the office, the bar is on two floors and comprises dining areas and more relaxed sofa spaces. For those who can't live without a financial fix, Bloomberg TV flickers in the corner. Wines cover an international range, and are described on the list which is compiled according to "body". As an alternative to the traditional wine bar prevalent in the City, Lime definitely rewards the adventurous drinker.

One of Two

45 Old Broad Street, EC2
020 7588 4845
Mon-Fri: 11am - 11pm
10 @ £2.90 - £4.00
24 @ £11.50 - £110.00

Upbeat downtown

If the standard City wine bar holds no attractions and you would prefer something more lively, One of Two offers a solution. On the corner of Wormwood Street, the bar appears almost incongruous in its high-rise surroundings. Outdoor seating on two levels precedes a three-tiered bar and dining space, laid out in minimalist style. A monumental up-lit shelving unit backs the bar, and on first inspection the spirit bottles displayed here (and the very loud chart music) might make you question One of Two's credentials as a place to drink serious wine. However the list dispels any fears, and there is a pleasing international selection, including curiosities such as "Fat Bastard" Chardonnay which might appeal to the 'wide' fraternity. Ideal for the young at heart.

Pacific Oriental

1 Bishopsgate, EC2
020 7621 9988
Mon-Fri: 11.30am - 11pm
7 @ £2.95 - £5.95
23 @ £11.95 - £53.50

Microbrewery springs wine surprise

While the pull of Pacific Oriental centres around its copper brewing vats, it does not forget the wine drinker in its efforts to appeal to a wide clientele. The expansive bar just below street level splits into different areas, and it's the ideal place to meet a group of friends after work. Staff are charming and helpful, and the glass sculptures of Pacific waves on the wall behind the long bar successfully evoke the daydream of chilling out in the tropics. Wines available on the bar list have been carefully chosen to offer an international choice. Those who wish to delve into fine wines are welcome to ask for the restaurant list from upstairs.

The Papermill

2-6 Curtain Road, EC2
020 7377 1606
Mon-Fri: 9am - 11pm
8 @ £2.80 - £4.90
34 @ £10.20 - £110.00

Wine in a warehouse

North of Liverpool Street station, Curtain Road leads into up and coming Shoreditch, fast developing a reputation for some of the hottest bars, clubs and eateries in London. The Papermill is one of the first you will come across, built into the ground floor of a former warehouse. Its relaxed atmosphere and varied spacious seating areas make it particularly good for groups who want to unwind, enjoy some drinks and perhaps a dish or two from the self-styled "eclectic mix" on the menu. The wine list is international, and helpfully split up into House, New World and Old World sections, with a brief description of each bottle to help you make your choice.

The Spitz Bar

Spitalfields Market, 109 Commercial Street, E1
020 7247 9747
Mon-Sat: 11am - 11pm
Sun: 11am - 10.30pm
4 @ £2.40 - £3.40
27 @ £9.25 - £60.00

Cool for cats

Amidst the remnants of Spitalfields market, the Spitz bar is a cool oasis drawing a youthful crowd from far and wide. Basic décor, young staff and fabulous food are topped off by a limited but interesting array of wines. Fans of French cinema, and especially of Gérard Depardieu, should come here to try the wine from his vineyard (Château de Tigne, £13.45 a bottle). Other unusual choices include a Malbec from Mexico, Verdicchio from Italy and a Petite Sirah from the US, amongst more traditional European offerings. The Spitz is also a venue for live music, particularly jazz, and is a great spot for a private party.
www.spitz.co.uk

Twenty-Four

Tower 42, 25 Old Broad Street, EC2
020 7877 2424
Mon-Fri: 11.45am - 11pm
8 @ £4.00 - £5.50
99 @ £13.95 - £239.00

Room with a view

You will find this small relaxed bar (and adjoining restaurant) the eponymous twenty-four floors above the City, past a welter of security checks which mean that you must phone ahead to make a booking. Any feelings of intimidation from this initial hurdle soon evaporate; the staff in the bar are welcoming and will do everything to make sure that your high-rise experience is a memorable pleasure. The view provides all the interest you could want, and décor is muted, with suede stools and armchairs set back from the windows so everyone can see their share of the panorama. Inevitably the location and the restriction on numbers puts a premium on the drinks, but there will be something to suit every pocket. This is no ordinary bar so why not treat yourself?

Vertigo

Tower 42, 25 Old Broad Street, EC2
020 7877 7842
Mon-Fri: Noon - 3pm/5pm - 11pm
10 @ £4.75 - £10.50
32 @ £18.95 - £175.00

Room with an even better view

More Champagne than you can shake a stick at, with magnums, Jeroboams and a stupendously-priced non-vintage Nebuchadnezzar at £1425.00, stake Vertigo's claim to be one of the best bars in London for fizzy pop. It's a narrow room perched on the edge of the lift shafts at the top of Tower 42, with table service only, and requiring advance booking in the same way as Twenty-Four does (see previous entry). Various seafood titbits are available to help soak up the Champagne, or one of the very small selection of non-sparkling wines on the list. If you want to make an impression, there's nothing quite like Vertigo; just make sure any guests have a head for heights before getting into the lift.

Plus:

All Bar One
18-20 Appold Street, EC2
020 7377 9671

Balls Brothers
158 Bishopsgate, EC2
020 7426 0567

Balls Brothers
11 Blomfield Street, EC2
020 7588 4643

Bangers (Davy's)
Eldon House, 2-12 Wilson Street, EC2
020 7377 6326

Chez Gérard
64 Bishopsgate, EC2
020 7588 1200

City House (Young's)
86 Bishopsgate, EC2
020 7628 3371

Corney & Barrow
19 Broadgate Circle, EC2
020 7628 1251

Corney & Barrow
5 Exchange Square, Broadgate, EC2
020 7628 4367

Dirty Dick's (Young's)
202 Bishopsgate, EC2
020 7283 5888

Grapeshots (Davy's)
2-3 Artillery Passage, E1
020 7247 8215

Jamies
155 Bishopsgate, EC2
020 7256 7279

The Orangery (Jamies)
10 Devonshire Square, EC2
020 7623 1377

Pitcher & Piano
200 Bishopsgate, EC2
020 7929 5914

The Blue-Eyed Maid

173 Borough High Street, SE1
020 7378 8259
Mon-Fri: 11am - 11pm
15 @ £2.25 - £5.00
15 @ £8.50 - £15.00

Wine list looks to Italy for inspiration

This cosy modernised pub is a local favourite, an easy stroll down Borough High Street. The front door is off a little alley, opening on to the bar which takes pride of place half-way down the narrow room. Seating is in two main areas either side of the bar, and big wall mirrors create the illusion of space. The wine is racked impressively on high shelves behind the bar. Blue and cream décor with wooden tables and chairs gives the place a mellow feel, ideal for a quiet chat over a drink or some food. Being further away from London Bridge the clientele is more mixed and the atmosphere less City-fied. The wine selection, though limited, offers something to accommodate most tastes – and at reasonable prices.

Cantina Vinopolis

1 Bank End, London SE1
020 7645 3700
Mon-Sun: 11am - 10.30pm
100+ @ £2.50 upwards.
113 @ £11.50 upwards.

Wine wonderland

The Cantina at Vinopolis is the perfect venue to visit if you are feeling adventurous, and want to try some wines that you have either never tried or never even heard of before. The fact that every wine on the list (and there are over one hundred still wines, plus Champagne, sparkling wines, ports and dessert wines) is available by two sizes of glass, as well as by the bottle, means that experimentation is actively encouraged. The wine list is organised varietally rather than by region, and has a brief tasting note beside each entry. You are bound to find something that you like! If you are in the area, why not drop in and try it out?

Cooperage

48-50 Tooley Street, SE1
020 7403 5775
Mon-Tue: 11am - 9pm
Wed-Fri: 11am - 11pm
16 @ £2.85 - £5.00
33 @ £11.25 - £49.95

Home is where the hearth is

Tooley Street runs parallel to the river between London Bridge and HMS Belfast, and the Cooperage is exactly what it says it is: a barrel-making forge (now transformed into a wine bar). One of three Davy's establishments in the street, it is worth walking past the other two on a chilly day to enjoy the cosy fire which crackles in the old hearth. Cooping equipment hangs on the walls, and Davy's trademark sawdust covers the floor. The bar menu comprises hearty sandwiches and salads, with a dining menu also available. The wines are mainly from Davy's own sources, but the range is wide and they always have special offers for curious drinkers. A decent choice of sherry and port completes the list.
www.davy.co.uk

Heeltap & Bumper

White Hart Yard, SE1
020 7407 2829
Mon-Fri: 11am - 11pm
16 @ £2.70 - £4.95
29 @ £10.50 - £43.50

Illustrious neighbours

White Hart Yard is one of many such courtyards reached by ducking down an alley off Borough High Street. This is allegedly Shakespeare and Dickens territory, and the Heeltap & Bumper is in fact opposite the George Inn, supposedly one of the Bard's haunts. Whatever the truth, you can be sure you are in one of the oldest parts of London. The Heeltap suffers slightly by comparison with its illustrious neighbour, but offers spacious seating, including sofas and easy chairs, in a light and airy room. It has a comprehensive international wine list, as befits its background as a Davy's café-bar, making it a pleasant alternative to one of the many local pubs.
www.davy.co.uk

Hop Cellars

24 Southwark Street, SE1
020 7403 6851
Mon-Fri: 11.30am - 8.30pm
10 @ £3.30 - £4.50
82 @ £13.00 - £120.00

Style and tradition

Downstairs under the 19th century Hop Exchange in London's Borough, this is a classic Balls Brothers wine bar. Character prints and wine memorabilia (corkscrews and large empty Champagne bottles a speciality), combined with an imposing dark wooden bar across the back wall, give the impression of quality and tradition with which the chain is associated. The wine list is predominantly French, including the inevitable Champagne, hence the most expensive bottle price. This is complemented by some well-chosen international selections, as well as bin ends and fine wines. Hop Cellars also runs events for wine-lovers throughout the year, as do other Balls Brothers bars across London.
www.ballsbrothers.co.uk

Our Cellar

King's Head Yard, SE1
020 7407 3451
Mon-Fri: Noon - 11pm
9 @ £2.50 - £3.50
36 @ £8.50 - £35.00

"In Vino Felicitas"

Such is the motto ("In wine lies happiness") inscribed on the list of this curious wine bar-restaurant. Down some narrow stairs behind a non-descript doorway off Borough High Street (on the left as you walk away from the river), the overall theme is Italian. The basement room is packed full of mementoes of the old country, and the reasonably-priced wine list reflects the Latinate origins of both the cooking and the staff. There is a decent nod to the rest of the world's wines too. While the décor has not changed since time began, the welcome is warm and the customers were more than complimentary about their lunch. Well worth keeping your eyes peeled for, particularly if you relish the prospect of fellow diners' genuine London accents with your pasta.

London Bridge

Wine Wharf

Stoney Street, SE1
020 7940 8335
Mon-Fri: 11am - 11pm
Sat: Noon - 11pm; Sun: Noon - 6pm
124+ @ £3.20 - £24.95
210 @ £11.30 - £215.10

So many wines, so little time!

For sheer range and quality of wines it is virtually impossible to walk past this vinous paradise, behind Vinopolis on the Borough Market side of the railway arches. There are other places in London where the wine is more reasonably priced and the venue more traditional, but this is the wine-lovers' equivalent of letting a child loose in a sweet shop. Scrubbed-up original brickwork, offset with modern steel and wood, houses various seating areas including cushy sofas, and papers or magazines for after you have read the many wine lists. Wine Flights are available if you can't make up your mind. Whether a connoisseur or just starting out on your adventures with wine, you can't go far wrong in here.

Plus:

All Bar One

28-30 London Bridge Street, SE1
020 7940 9981

Balls Brothers

Hays Galleria, Tooley Street, SE1
020 7407 4301

Bunch of Grapes (Young's)

2 St Thomas Street, SE1
020 7403 2070

Mughouse (Davy's)

1-3 Tooley Street, SE1
020 7403 8344

Skinkers (Davy's)

42 Tooley Street, SE1
020 7407 9189

Mansion House

Bar Under the Clock

74 Queen Victoria Street, EC4
020 7489 9895
Mon-Fri: 11am - 11pm
12 @ £3.20 - £4.00
28 @ £12.50 - £100.00

For Whom the Bell Tolls

Part of the Balls Brothers chain, but not its usual 'traditional' style. This bar is literally under the church on Queen Victoria Street, and its hidden location makes it a snug little hideaway from the madness at street level. The subtly lit bar is bright and modern, with flagstone floors and the inevitable pale wood furniture. Arranged by price, the wine list is extensive, eclectic, and offers a good range of varietals from a number of countries. This is a good place to try something a little out of the ordinary. Special events and themed evenings mean that returning here time and time again need not feel like Groundhog Day.
www.ballsbrothers.co.uk

The College Press Wine Bar

10-11 College Hill, EC4
020 7489 9196
Mon-Fri: 11.30am - 10pm
12 @ £2.50 - £3.75
20 @ £9.95 - £49.95

Vinous study

Tucked down some stairs away from the roar of traffic on Upper Thames Street, the College Press is quite tricky to locate. Look for a pedestrian alleyway, and it's next door to a sandwich shop. This little bar is fun, friendly, and, if you can get past the local office crowd, is a cheery place to spend an evening. The wine list has a good range and is sure to have something for everyone, although don't come here looking for anything out of the ordinary. Safe, solid and teamed with hearty bar snacks, this is a place to keep in the back of your mind when in the area.

Mansion House

Heeltap & Bumper ⊖

2-6 Cannon Street, EC4
☎020 7248 3371
Mon-Fri: 11am - 11pm
🍷16 @ £2.75 - £5.35
🍾28 @ £10.95 - £43.50

Local crowd-pleaser

Almost opposite St Paul's Cathedral and close to the promenade leading to the Millennium Bridge, this bar is the perfect watering hole after a spot of sightseeing. It is a bright, busy, modern bar full of local office workers slaking their thirst after a hard day's graft and watching the sport on the huge screen adorning one wall. The wines offered here are classic, safe and likely to please most people, although there is nothing exciting to really stimulate the taste buds. Nevertheless, a good list for a non-specialist wine bar.
www.davy.co.uk

Plus:

Balls Brothers
Cannon Street, Budge Row, EC4
☎020 7248 7557

Corney & Barrow ⊖
44 Cannon Street, EC4
☎020 7248 1700

Jamies
5 Groveland Court, EC4
☎020 7248 5551

Pitcher & Piano
67-69 Watling Street, EC4
☎020 7248 0883

⊖ Monument

La Grande Marque

55 Leadenhall Market, EC3
☎020 7929 3536
Mon-Fri: 11am - 9pm
🍷17 @ £3.50 - £8.50
🍾104 @ £11.95 - £250.00

Wine Mecca in the Market

The sister bar to La Grande Marque on Ludgate Hill is a little trickier to find than its sibling. Go into the market by the southern entrance and take the first alley on the left. The bar is opposite Marina Café, down a flight of stairs. Once inside, the bar opens into a much larger space than first impressions would suggest. This underground cellar, with its exposed brick walls and ceiling and pine floors, is dedicated to the grape. The list is extensive and offers quaffers the opportunity to try out a wide variety of wines from all over the world. Top producers abound, and interestingly there are a number of wines offered in half bottles – perfect if you are being abstemious or simply want to experiment with several bottles. Don't miss it!

Monument

Leadenhall Colony Wine Bar

9 Leadenhall Market, EC3

☎020 7283 5656

Mon-Fri: 11am - 9pm

14 @ £2.80 - £4.00

56 @ £10.90 - £98.00

Market force

Part of the mini-chain of Colony wine bars, Leadenhall Colony is found on the first floor of the market, up some stairs behind a fairly unprepossessing entrance. There are no surprises once in the bar; the wine list is the same as in the other Colonies, with a solid offering of international bottles and a selection of fine wines. The welcome is genuine and friendly, and the clientele is well and truly able to relax in a laid-back, comfortable environment. A safe bet!

Leadenhall Wine and Tapas Bar

27 Leadenhall Market, EC3

☎020 7625 1818

Mon-Fri: 11.30am - 11pm

34 @ £2.85 - £8.95

41 @ £10.45 - £69.95

Olé!

A favourite haunt, if you can judge by the number of approved stickers on the door, this tapas bar is upstairs within the market, close to the Lloyds Building entrance. A large, airy, circular room with big windows overlooks the bustle of the market below, making this a pleasant venue to quaff wine and have a bite to eat. Staff are friendly and attentive and almost all the wines are available by the glass, so you can pick and choose to suit the mood or the dish. The list is interesting and varied, and at the time of visiting had absolutely no French wines to choose from. Spanish wines dominate as expected, but there are offerings from Italy, Chile, Australia, Argentina and South Africa to provide an international perspective.

Plus:

Balls Brothers

52 Lime Street, EC3

☎020 7283 0841

Balls Brothers

2 St Mary at Hill, EC3

☎020 7626 0321

Bangers Too (Davy's)

1 St Mary at Hill, EC3

☎020 7283 4443

Bill Bentley's by the Monument (Young's)

1 St George's Lane, EC3

☎020 7929 2244

City F.O.B. (Davy's)

Lower Thames Street, EC3

☎020 7621 0619

Corney & Barrow at Lloyd's of London

1, Leadenhall Place, EC3

☎020 7621 9201

Corney & Barrow at the Monument

2b Eastcheap, EC3

☎020 7929 3220

El Vino

The Old Wine Shades, 6 Martin Lane, EC4

☎020 7626 6876

The Fine Line

Equitable House, 1 Monument Street, EC3

☎020 7623 5446

Jamies

13 Philpot Lane

☎020 7621 9577

Lamb Tavern (Young's)

10-12 Leadenhall Market, EC3

☎020 7626 2454

The Walrus and Carpenter (Young's)

45 Monument Street, EC3

☎020 7626 3362

Finch's

12a Finsbury Square, EC2
☎020 7588 3311
Mon-Fri: 11am - 11pm
28 @ £2.75 - £5.00
35 @ £11.85 - £45.00

A bird in the hand

Young's Brewery ventures into the world of upmarket modern style with its Finch's bars, here in the City, in Fulham and in Wimbledon. The green of the square opposite is almost enough to make you forget the urban location. Named after one of London's oldest pub companies, there is little else to remind customers of the past. Contemporary colours and smart, comfortable furnishings provide a relaxed ambience in which to enjoy an extensive selection of wines, particularly by the glass. The list describes the wines' character with mouth-watering adjectives, and the range is international and moderately priced, especially by City standards. Finch's is perfect for a business lunch or an after-work drink with friends, with wines to match.

The Pavilion

Finsbury Circus, EC2
☎020 7628 8224
Mon-Fri: 11.30am - 11.30pm
38 @ £3.40 - £8.00
67 @ £13.65 - £125.00

Wine in the round

This Jamies establishment enjoys a lush aspect overlooking the bowling green in the middle of the Circus. The gardens are the oldest in the City, and the unique location provides unexpected relief from the busy thoroughfare of London Wall just a few metres away. The bar itself is cosy, and offers the standard Jamies selection of reliable international wines, with a decent range of Champagnes (including magnums and a Jeroboam for special celebrations). It's hard to beat such a verdant oasis when all around is stone or concrete, and with the Jamies wine list as an added incentive, it could be time to make your excuses and spend some time in the Pavilion.

Plus:

All Bar One
127 Finsbury Pavement, EC2
☎020 7448 9921

The Bishop of Norwich (Davy's)
91-93 Moorgate, EC2
☎020 7920 0857

Bishop's Parlour (Davy's)
91-93 Moorgate, EC2
☎020 7588 2581

City Boot (Davy's)
7 Moorfields High Walk, EC2
☎020 7588 4766

Corney & Barrow
12 Mason's Avenue, EC2
☎020 7726 6030

Corney & Barrow at CityPoint
1 Ropemaker Street, EC2
☎020 7448 3700

El Vino
Bastion High Walk, 125 London Wall, EC2
☎020 7600 6377

Heeltap & Bumper
2-4 Paul Street, EC2
☎020 7247 3319

The Pulpit (Davy's)
63 Worship Street, EC2
☎020 7377 1574

Mornington Crescent

El Parador

245 Eversholt Street, NW1
☎020 7387 2789
Mon-Thu: Noon - 3pm/6pm - 11pm
Fri: Noon - 3pm/6pm - 11.30pm
Sat: 6pm - 11.30pm; Sun: 7pm - 10.30pm
10 @ £2.80 - £3.80
27 @ £10.00 - £20.00

Authentic selection

Here for fourteen years, El Parador brings a touch of Spanish authenticity to North London. The bar is a short walk back towards the city from the station, and is located in a cosy space which could just as easily be found in Barcelona or Madrid. Calm blues are complemented by a sparkly Gaudi-influenced bar front, and there is a pretty courtyard at the back in which to escape from the traffic outside. The wine list is exclusively Hispanic, mostly from Iberia but with some South American bottles for good measure. There are also several sherries by the glass. The licence here requires that you eat in order to drink, but the reasonably-priced tapas selection is so appetising that this is no hardship.

192 Bar & Restaurant

192 Kensington Park Road, W11
☎020 7229 0482
Mon-Sat: 12.30pm - 11pm
Sun: 12.30pm - 10.30pm
28 @ £2.90 - £6.60
83 @ £10.50 - £95.00

Have some chutzpah handy

192 is a place whose name pops up in celebrity interviews, which gives an indication of the clientele. However, staff here will only go so far as to say that they have their 'regulars', and if you want a table at certain times of day it helps to be a familiar face (preferably eating). Refreshing honesty, if not brilliant marketing, but the quality wine list is hard to ignore, and at quieter moments this really is a pleasant place to call into for a drink or two. The Old World predominates, but coverage is broad and impressive regardless. Portobello Road market runs in the parallel street, and the whole area is alive with specialist shops and fascinating people. Get into the mix, brave the cool exterior of 192, and be rewarded with friendly service and an excellent wine choice.

The Chepstow

39 Chepstow Place, W2
☎020 7229 0323
Mon-Sat: Noon - 11pm
Sun: Noon - 10.30pm
8 @ £2.50 - £3.25
25 @ £9.95 - £58.50

Cunningly disguised

In possibly the last place that you would expect to find a pub, The Chepstow is camouflaged by the façades of surrounding town houses. Approaching through quiet streets from the Tube, the only signs of its existence are a couple of hanging baskets out front and the name over the door. Inside a light, spacious room, the Chepstow has the art of the British gastropub down pat: modern European cooking, with a full range of beverages to match. The wine list shows a classic international selection, with some well-known producers featured. With the options for drinking wine in this area somewhat limited, seeking out the Chepstow is time well spent.
www.massivepub.com

The Wine Factory

294 Westbourne Grove, W11
020 7229 1877
Mon-Sat: Noon - 3.30pm/6pm - 11pm
Sun: 11am - 4pm
None listed
40 @ £5.00 - £37.50

Bargains to be had

Yes, that's a genuine lowest price per bottle, because this venue (belonging to the Brinkley's mini-chain of restaurants and brasseries) cuts out the middle man and sells wine at retail prices to lucky customers, rather than imposing a healthy mark-up. The Wine Factory has a restaurant licence so you will have to eat something in order to drink, but it seems a shame not to share news about value for money. Take your pick from a selection which concentrates on France but does not neglect international favourites. The proximity to Portobello Road market makes this a great place to fortify yourself before or after some serious haggling, and the money you save on wine will allow you to make that indulgent purchase with a clear conscience.

Plus:

All Bar One

126-128 Notting Hill, W11
020 7313 9362

Café Med

184a Kensington Park Road, W11
020 7221 1150

The Duke of Wellington (Young's)

179 Portobello Road, W11
020 7727 6727

Cantaloupe Bar & Grill

35 Charlotte Road, Shoreditch, EC2
020 7729 5566
Mon-Sat: 11.30am - Midnight
Sun: 11am - 11.30pm
11 @ £2.50 - £5.00
40 @ £9.50 - £69.00

No frills but plenty of front

As with many of the new bars and clubs in Shoreditch, Cantaloupe has been created inside a former industrial space, in this case some kind of warehouse. Eclectic seating includes studded leather sofas and armchairs, benches made from scaffolding poles and railway sleepers, chairs created from packing boxes, and lots of other things which could have come from your Gran's house clearance. This is the antithesis of a themed space, which makes it very easy to relax and enjoy one of the excellent Old or New World wines on the blackboard list above the bar. Tasty tapas-style food complements the wine selection.
www.cantaloupe.co.uk

Cargo

Kingsland Viaduct, 83 Rivington Street, EC2
020 7739 3440
Mon-Fri: Noon - 1am
Sat: 6pm - 1am; Sun: Noon - Midnight
27 @ £2.50 - £6.30
29 @ £9.50 - £80.00

Who said clubs and wine don't mix?

Strictly speaking, Cargo is a club, hence the late closing times. It sells itself as a provider of "MDF" (not the TV DIY essential, rather music, drink, food) and does all three with some style. Built into space under the railway, there are several distinct areas which use texture rather than colour to give them a personality. Try carpet on some of the walls, concrete, brick, and a corner with inviting velvety cushions piled up and just asking to be dived into (but put your drink down first). It's dimly lit, no doubt to maintain the ambience, so this is not a place to appreciate the appearance of a wine. On the other hand, you don't need daylight to enjoy a wine's taste, and the list here includes an impressive international range.

The Firehouse Cellars

140 Tabernacle Street, EC2
☎020 7490 2962
Mon-Fri: 11.30am - 10pm
7 @ £2.80 - £3.70
56 @ £11.50 - £120.00

Hot favourite

At the north end of Tabernacle Street, the former Old Street fire station retains vestiges of its former incarnation, most notably bright red paintwork. Down metal stairs painted the same colour, offset by wrought iron vines, you will find the Firehouse Cellars, full of wine memorabilia and firemen's sayings. Among all the newfound cool of Shoreditch, it's a pleasant surprise to find an old-fashioned wine den, buzzing with vitality. With an emphasis on French and Italian wines, the management is keen to spread the word that the Cellars provides good service and value for money relatively near the City. Judging by the happy lunchtime crowd packing the bar, this is a widely-known fact already.

CJ's

12 City Road, Finsbury Square, EC1
☎020 7638 1324
Mon-Fri: 8.30am - 11pm
12 @ £2.80 - £5.50
60 @ £9.80 - £69.00

City original

Here for twenty years, CJ's was the first bar on the square, and its relaxed charm shows that it doesn't need to prove anything to the local bars which have followed in its wake. Photos behind the bar reveal its popularity as a haunt for regulars, but there's also a warm welcome for newcomers and those who roll up from the City. A long thin room has the bar near the front and a light, bright dining area at the far end. MTV (silent during the day) and papers are provided for customers. The wines are carefully chosen by the owners, and represent a decent international selection which will not break the bank.
www.cjsbar.co.uk

Great Eastern Dining Room

54-56 Great Eastern Street, EC2
☎020 7613 4545
Mon-Fri: Noon - Midnight
Sat: 6pm - Midnight
11 @ £2.50 - £7.00
58 @ £10.00 - £89.00

Sets standards for Shoreditch style

Set in the ground floor of a former warehouse, the Great Eastern Dining Room dominates the junction with Charlotte Road. The exterior doesn't give much away, with ribbed glass lower window panes obscuring any curious glances from the street. Brave the unknown though, and you enter a spacious bar which has banquettes around the edges, plus lots of standing room and tables. It's consciously cool with '50s-influenced style, but this doesn't prevent it being a comfortable spot in which to join friends, run a business meeting or sit quietly with a book. The fairly-priced bar wine list is relatively short, but with the dining room adjacent, it's no trouble to see the full selection of international choices.

Home

100-106 Leonard Street, EC2
☎020 7684 8618
Mon-Sat: 5pm - 11.30pm
11 @ £3.00 - £4.50
41 @ £12.50 - £90.00

Smarter than the average living room

At the Great Eastern Street end of the road, Home occupies three former shops, giving it huge picture windows for seeing and being seen. Divided into two main spaces, this is another Shoreditch special in the bar-dining room mould. Here the food takes pride of place in a chic dining room at street level, while drinkers will find a more relaxed atmosphere below stairs. Attracting a varied clientele of all ages, the immediate impression is that you have arrived among the 'Beautiful People', which might be a little intimidating. Life's too short to worry about such hang-ups, so don't let anything stop you from checking out a wide-ranging international wine selection which will suit all pockets.
www.homebar.co.uk

Katabatic

89 Great Eastern Street, EC2
☎020 7739 5173
Mon-Wed: 11am - 11pm
Thu: 11am - 1am; Fri & Sat: 11am - 3am
4 @ £2.90 - £3.80
20 @ £11.50 - £110.00

Chill with the fishes

With an imaginative take on modern bar stylings, Katabatic has a maritime theme which holds everything together but doesn't overwhelm. The main bar has a long curving counter with three tropical fishtanks featured behind it, there's a small mezzanine dining space, and downstairs a club dancefloor. The weary can rest their legs by sitting on some of the funkiest furniture in London. The whole effect is as close to the tranquillity of diving as you're likely to get on dry land. Katabatic is a great venue for winding down alone or with friends, and doesn't seem to carry any pretentious overtones. This extends to the wine list, where reputable international names rub shoulders at reasonable prices.

The Liquid Lab

20 City Road, EC1
☎020 7920 0372
Mon-Fri: 11am - 11pm
10 @ £2.50 - £7.95
32 @ £10.50 - £95.00

Clinical excellence

Just up from Finsbury Square, the Liquid Lab pursues the medicinal theme but keeps it tongue-in-cheek. A long clean white space, with various specimens of tables and chairs, is enhanced with light boxes covered by humorous X-rays which have to be seen to be believed. If conversation fails, these will be sure to provoke a response! There is a small mezzanine area, and a couple of dentist's chairs lurk provocatively beyond the neon-lit bar. Whatever your poison and however you choose to ingest it, the friendly staff at the Liquid Lab can prescribe it. For wine-lovers, the list is international and eclectic, with brief descriptions provided. Worth a visit just to experience the original setting.

Plus:

Colonel Jasper's (Davy's)

190 City Road, EC1
☎020 7608 0925

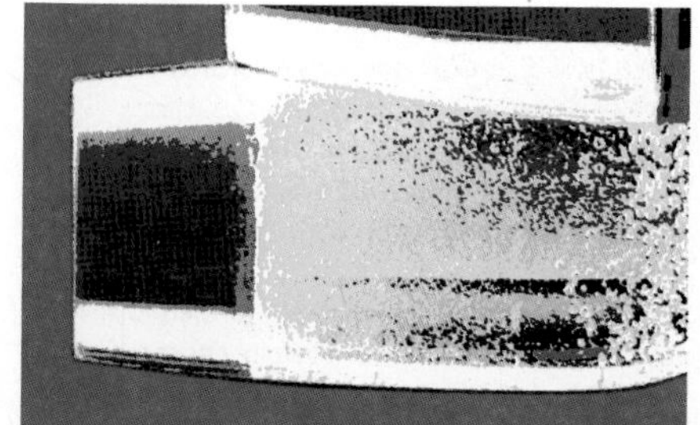

Ha!Ha! Bar & Canteen

43 Great Titchfield Street, W1
020 7580 7252
Mon-Fri: 10am - 11pm
7 @ £2.80 - £3.00
15 @ £11.50 - £37.50

Confident bar-chain choice

Extremely popular with local workers and media types, the Ha!Ha! is a good example of a modern bar mini-chain which sells a lifestyle as much as food and drink. Look beyond the own-brand condiments and other bits and pieces, and you will find a relaxed, friendly place split into a dining and bar area. The latter has huge picture windows (it's on a corner a small distance up from Oxford Street), formula sofas and low tables, and a proliferation of zinc-topped counters at which to sip from one of the select range of wines. These are not numerous, but they do represent reasonable quality without springing any surprises. Ha!Ha! offers a complete package which is worth investigating if you're in the area.
www.hahaonline.co.uk

Hanover Square Wine Bar & Grill

25 Hanover Square, W1
020 7408 0935
Mon-Fri: 11am - 11pm
24 @ £3.00 - £6.00
182 @ £11.50 - £235.00

"Life's too short to drink bad wine."

By this dictum shall ye know the mission of bar owner Don Hewitson, and here is a place to put his theory to the test. A sandwich board announcing the bar's location sits at the top of metal stairs which lead down to the basement of a large office block. This is a big brick space, painted dark red, with ferns and ivy peeking out from planters between the ceiling beams. A bar and food servery occupy the far wall, and blackboards are jammed in between wine posters to advertise food and wine specials. The wine selection is nothing short of stupendous, so grab a table down here and make the most of some genuine treasures of both the Old and New Worlds.
www.donhewitsonlondonwinebars.co.uk

Maddox Street Wine Bar

12-14 Maddox Street, W1
020 7941 2424
Mon-Thu: Noon - 11pm
Fri: Noon - 1am; Sat: 7pm - 1am
12 @ £2.60 - £4.95
39 @ £11.00 - £190.00

Star bar

The owner of Maddox Street is very proud of his record as erstwhile host to some of London's celebrity faces, and has a photo board near the bar to prove it. Drawn to this bright and spacious downstairs room just off Regent Street, the majority of customers tend to be office workers during the week and clubbers at the weekend. Whatever their origin, they can enjoy an international wine list which contains bottles from well-known producers as well as some more unusual quaffs. The bar menu caters for all appetites throughout the day, and there are several themed nights each week offering salsa, disco, soul and R'n'B.
www.maddoxstreetwinebar.com

Needles Wine Bar

5-6 Clipstone Street, W1
020 7436 0035
Mon-Fri: 11.30am - 11pm
5 @ £2.50 - £3.25
27 @ £9.60 - £39.50

True to tradition

Just off Great Portland Street, Needles is another in the traditional mould of basement wine bars: parquet floor, large mirror tiles on pillars, chunky pub-style tables and chairs, wooden bar with a couple of pot-plants and the wine glasses hanging from a rack system above. As is often the case with such places, there is a dedicated clientele which recognises when it's on to a good thing, and returns again and again. Here, the wine list is international but France features several times; there is also a decent selection of aperitifs and liqueurs to complement the list.

Oxford Circus

Shampers Wine Bar & Restaurant

4 Kingly Street, W1
☎020 7437 1692
Mon-Sat: 11am - 11pm
26 @ £2.95 - £5.00
162 @ £11.50 - £120.00

Alternative retail therapy

Kingly Street runs parallel to Regent Street, with Liberty's at one end and Shampers Wine Bar at the other. But why shop when you can come to this delightful establishment and partake of one of the best wine selections in town? A dark-green painted room has dining tables at the front and an informal bar area at the rear, wine is racked overhead, and mirrors create the illusion of greater space. Service is impeccable, and it's small touches such as tablecloths and fresh flowers which add even more to the civilised ambience. The wine list is extremely impressive, covering a full international range at exceptional prices, and reflecting the management's aim to provide customers with wines to enjoy without paying the earth.

Plus:

All Bar One

3-4 Hanover Street, W1
☎020 7518 9931

All Bar One

289-293 Regent Street, W1
☎020 7467 9901

Chopper Lump (Davy's)

10c Hanover Square, W1
☎020 7499 7569

Jamies

58-59 Poland Street, W1
☎020 7287 6666

Lees Bag (Davy's)

4 Great Portland Street, W1
☎020 7636 5287

Pitcher & Piano

10 Pollen Street, W1
☎020 7629 9581

The Windmill (Young's)

6-8 Mill Street, W1
☎020 7491 8050

Paddington

The Reef

Paddington Station Concourse, W2
☎020 7402 1599
Mon-Sat: 7am - 11pm
Sun: 8am - 10.30pm
10 @ £2.40 - £3.35
12 @ £8.80 - £36.00

No train? No pain

Ever had that sinking feeling: the train is late, the person you are waiting for is on it, or worse still, you are delayed yourself? Fear not! If you are a wine drinker, Paddington Station has provided for you at the Reef with a more than acceptable selection of quick quaffs which should help to ease the stress brought on by the vagaries of the British railway system. This is modern station café writ large, with the usual tables and chairs, plus comfortable sofas, and aquaria to transfix the most agitated traveller into a brief spell of calm. While the wines won't set records for imagination, they are a welcome addition to the buffet menu. If this is the future of public transport catering, waiting for that train won't be so aggravating after all. Also at Victoria and Waterloo Stations.

Plus:

Gyngleboy (Davy's)

27 Spring Street, W2
☎020 7723 3351

Ciao Bistro & Bar

222 Munster Road, SW6
☎020 7381 6137
Mon-Sat: 11am - 11pm
Sun: Noon - 10.30pm
11 @ £2.75 - £4.95
130 @ £11.00 - £35.00

Fulham favourite

On the corner of Munster and Orbain Roads, Ciao is divided into a light, airy drinking area and a more formal dining space. A pavement terrace adds continental ambience for warm days, and inside, light colours and a parquet floor evoke Mediterranean summers. An unusual collection of paintings of angels (belonging to the owner) are certain to provoke comment. A variety of grapes is represented on the internationally-influenced wine list, ideal to accompany something from the modern European menu. The effort required to get to this part of town for non-locals makes this a place to relax and enjoy a whole evening, an attractive enough proposition in surroundings as relaxed as these.

Sydney

199 Munster Road, SW6
☎020 7381 8821
Mon-Fri: Noon - 11pm
Sat: 11am - 11pm; Sun: 11am - 10.30pm
17 @ £3.50 - £4.95 (250ml)
124 @ £9.95 - £45.00

No worries

A little piece of Australia on a sunny corner in Fulham, Sydney is chock-a-block with photos and posters of Down Under. It's just down from the Lillie Road junction, so a healthy hike from the Tube, but there are local bus services which will ease the journey. Bright paintwork and pavement tables foster the illusion of southern summers, and the food menu contains Pacific Rim specials such as kangaroo and a pleasing choice of fish dishes. Sadly the wine list does not truly reflect the riches of the Australian industry, sticking instead to a routine international selection. A missed opportunity in this respect, but otherwise the relaxed Antipodean atmosphere makes this a pleasant place to while away the time.
www.sydneybrasseries.co.uk

Parson's Green

The White Horse

1-3 Parson's Green, SW6
☎020 7736 2115
Mon-Sat: 11am - 11pm
Sun: 11am - 10.30pm
8 @ £2.85 - £3.75
149 @ £10.75 - £48.00

Wonderful wines out West

Rather cruelly dubbed the "Sloaney Pony", this shouldn't put you off from visiting this large pub on the edge of the Green. It attracts more than the regulation Fulhamites, and if you are vaguely serious about wine you would be foolish to miss it. The White Horse retains some of the genuine charm of old-style pubs, with benches, big tables and leather sofas – none of which looks like it has been shipped in from the authentic pub factory – but has food and drink for the 21st century. The wine list impresses with an eclectic international selection to suit all pockets, including treats from the Rhône, Western Australia, several Italians and even some German choices. Port, sherry and dessert wines are not forgotten either.

Plus:

The Duke of Cumberland (Young's)

235 New King's Road, SW6
☎020 7736 2777

Pitcher & Piano

871-873 Fulham Road, SW6
☎020 7736 3910

Le Bar du Marché

19 Berwick Street, Soho, W1
020 7734 4606
Mon-Sat: 11am - 11.30pm
8 @ £2.60 - £4.50
19 @ £10.00 - £38.95

Vrai Français

Deep in the heart of Soho is one of London's many street markets, fruit and flower stalls in the middle of the road, and here at least, fabulous fabric shops which stock all kinds of everything in textiles. The Bar du Marché is full of local characters, reading papers, sipping coffee, tucking in to one of the daily menu specials and quaffing wine. French is the house language and the house style, so the wines are in keeping (though you will find a couple of Spanish and Australian guests on the list or as one of the monthly specials). This lively bar wouldn't be out of place on the Left Bank in Paris, but fortunately for London it's a lot nearer than that.

Bentley's Cabin Bar

11-15 Swallow Street, W1
020 7734 4756
Mon-Sat: Noon - 11.30pm
10 @ £2.75 - £6.50
22 @ £10.75 - £105.00

Basement bolthole

Bentley's Cabin Bar is situated in this quiet alley off Regent Street not far up from the Tube, in a basement next to the Bentley's seafood restaurant. The bar is spacious with flagged floors and candlelight enhances its tranquil atmosphere. The selection of wines is not large, but there is a refreshing mix of varietals from several New and Old world countries. The staff here are French and the food is good bar menu fare. A great little bolthole, particularly after a spot of West End shopping or before going on to the theatre.

Daniel's Wine Bar (Café Royal)

9 Glasshouse Street, London W1
0870 400 8686
Mon-Sat: 11am - 10pm
11 @ £2.90 - £7.50
37 @ £13.75 - £132.00

Colonial splendour

Approached either from Glasshouse Street or from the Café Royal entrance at 68 Regent Street, Daniel's has refined elegance and an air of tranquility about it. Wicker chairs, ceiling fans and discreetly piped jazz all help to transport the drinker back to the '20s, though the modern bar jolts you back into the 21st century. Daniel's has an attractive wine list by the bottle, but only a rather limited selection by the glass. Nevertheless it's a pleasant spot to while away an hour or two, and the location between Piccadilly Circus and Soho will appeal to a varied clientele.

Hampton's Wine Bar

15 Whitcomb Street, WC2
020 7839 2823
Mon-Fri: 11.30am - 11pm
13 @ £2.90 - £7.00
59 @ £10.75 - £75.00

Hidden bargains

At the south end of the street, Hampton's is the epitome of late '70s/early '80s wine bar: large open space, quarry tiled floor, bistro-style tables and chairs, respectable list featuring French wines but covering all the international bases as well. The bar is slightly off the beaten track, so tends to be populated by local office workers who know where to find it. Hampton's doesn't have a great deal of individual style, but making the trek into the maze of small streets and alleys off Pall Mall will be rewarded with a decent glass or bottle and hearty food, below standard West End prices.

Piccadilly Circus

L'Odéon

65 Regent Street, W1
☎020 7287 1400
Mon-Sat: Noon - Midnight
13 @ £3.80 - £6.90
80 @ £15.50 - £115.00

Watch the world go by

Upstairs in a series of the sweep of arches which line Regent Street, L'Odéon is the epitome of cool sophistication. Soft furnishings placed at discreet distances afford some intimacy, and if you can bag a table by the window you get an unrivalled outlook towards Piccadilly Circus. This place is about comfort more than crowds, for which you pay a relative premium on drinks. If financially challenged, you may need to save your visit for a really special occasion! The bar benefits from its companion restaurant within the same space, which means that the range of wines available is greater than it might otherwise be. There is a good selection of French bottles, complemented by some serious international contenders – just ask to see the full list.

The Studio Lounge (Waterstone's)

203 Piccadilly, W1
☎020 7851 2433
Mon-Sat: 11am - 11pm
Sun: Noon - 6pm
14 @ £2.95 - £7.50
15 @ £12.50 - £45.00

Book-lovers' bonus

London is not over-endowed with public spaces from which you can gain any sort of panoramic view, so the presence of a lounge bar on the 5th floor of Waterstone's bookshop (the largest in Europe) is a plus. Catch the lift up past all the books to a chic modern room which has a look of art gallery about it: white walls, sparse decoration, black and chrome furniture. The view, south over the rooftops of Whitehall and Westminster, more than compensates for the minimalist interior. Although the international wine list is as low-key as the décor, it has something suitable for most palates, and the rest of the food and drink menu is as diverse as the range of books outside in the shop.

Swallow Street Bar

12 Swallow Street, London W1
☎020 7287 9647
Mon-Sat: Noon - 1am
7 @ £3.50 - £6.50
11 @ £11.50 - £175.00

Design for life

A trendy venue just off Regent Street, this is a really funky bar. Optics are mounted on lighted coloured torches and a huge wave effect installation on the back wall should win an award for design. There are suede loungers, wooden tables and the wines are served in unusual and elegant glasses (which makes a refreshing change). The wine list seems to have been an afterthought as the emphasis is more on designer beers and spirits, but the selection is reasonable and safe enough as long as you're not after anything too spectacular to quaff.

Vigo's

11 Vigo Street, W1
☎020 7734 1947
Mon-Tue: 11am - 10pm
Wed-Fri: 11am - 11pm; Sat: Noon - 6pm
11 @ £2.50 - £3.35
11 @ £9.75 - £13.20

Cheap and cheerful

Perhaps not the most obvious place to go for a glass of wine, Vigo's nevertheless provides something that is otherwise lacking in the vicinity: moderate prices. Just off Regent Street on the way into Mayfair, it's really a pub which happens to serve several wines by both glass and bottle. None of these is spectacular but there is a range of varietals to choose from. If all you want is a quick break from shopping or the hordes of tourists outside, and maybe a light bar snack, brave the potted palms and faux '20s interior and let Vigo's do the rest.

Brahms Wine Bar Restaurant

147 Lupus Street, SW1
☎020 7233 9828
Mon-Sat: 11am - 11pm
Sun: 11am - 10.30pm
2 @ £2.45
126 @ £9.65 - £45.50

Neighbourhood favourite

At the Chelsea end of Lupus Street, Brahms originally had a musical theme, but the only vestige of this now is the name. Charming new owners have introduced a relaxed style to the décor, with warm yellow walls offsetting driftwood-framed mirrors and table tops set on hunks of tree trunk. Wines are of recent vintage and are helpfully described on the list which is international in range. Although the by-glass selection is severely limited, a well-priced bottle here won't break the bank. Locals recommend the food too, including roast lunch on Sundays. With not many weekend options available in or near Central London, Brahms is worth knowing about.

The Contented Vine

17 Sussex Street, SW1
☎020 7834 0044
Mon-Fri: 11am - 3pm/5pm - 11pm
Sun: 11am - 11pm
23 @ £3.00 - £5.75
82 @ £10.95 - £55.00

You'll be happy too

Next-door to a specialist wine merchant, the Contented Vine benefits from its neighbour to provide a fine wine selection which complements the extensive general list. The main selection is worldwide, with plenty of French choices, and includes some mid-'90s vintages. Drinkers and brasserie diners are seated around the sizeable bar or at tables, with regular art exhibitions lining the walls in a brightly-lit room. The staff are friendly and accommodating, helping to keep this venue popular with locals. It's a lively place, where you can have an audible conversation among the general chatter, yet still feel part of the scene.

Goya

34 Lupus Street, SW1
☎020 7976 5309
Mon-Sun: Noon - Midnight
5 @ £2.50
49 @ £ 9.00 - £35.00

Tapas and fine Spanish wine

Small but perfectly formed, Goya is a delightful find in the Pimlico Grid. On the corner of Lupus Street and Morton Terrace, the bar is shoe-horned into the bottom of a small hotel. Far from being a disadvantage, this allows the ambience inside to buzz, and it's often packed out. Big windows allow patrons to feel smug as they look out at Pimlico pedestrians who can't get a table. Customers have to eat in order to drink, although the owners are petitioning for a different licence which will overcome this requirement. This is no hardship though, as the tapas are delicious and inexpensive, and a simple garlic bread will suffice to satisfy the law. For those who prefer something other than the impressive selection of Spanish wines, there are six token French choices.

Plus:

The Morpeth Arms (Young's)

58 Millbank, SW1
☎020 7834 6442

Putney (Bridge/East)

The Blue Pumpkin

147 Upper Richmond Road, SW15
020 8780 3553
Mon-Sun: 10am - 10.30pm
11 @ £2.50 - £4.15
41 @ £9.95 - £41.95

A ball before Midnight

Just over the major road junction outside the railway station, the Blue Pumpkin is a bright and airy café-brasserie. Bold paint and wall art announces a lively, modern venue which caters for a wide range of customers, young and old alike. Seating is at tables in a room which extends some way back, and there is a comfortable-looking sofa near the bar too. The wine list provides a solid international selection with helpful descriptions, and is moderately priced. The Blue Pumpkin merits a visit en route to your final destination, or is a perfect spot for lunch and a few glasses of wine to keep the spirits lifted.
www.bluepumpkin.co.uk

Parisà Café Bar

146-148 Putney High Street, SW15
020 8785 3131
Mon-Fri: 8am - 11pm
Sun: 10am - 10.30pm
20 @ £2.50 - £9.00
250+ @ £8.00 - £69.00

Spoilt for choice

Parisà is almost opposite the Putney railway station and its plate glass window frontage, decorated with a buxom serving wench, will ensure it cannot be passed by unnoticed. Inside this spacious venue, there is a 'writing on the walls' theme with quotes and cartoons emblazoned across the paint work. Modern décor and wooden tables and chairs complete the scene, and although Parisà sells itself as a café-bar, wine takes pride of place on its menu. Over 250 international wines are available, listed by country, with France and Australia sporting the largest range. There should be something here for everyone, and all are good value. The bar also sells wine to take home, if you fancy continuing to quaff in the comfort of your own surrounds.

Plus:

The Castle (Young's)

220 Putney Bridge Road, SW15
020 8788 0972

The Spotted Horse (Young's)

122 Putney High Street, SW15
020 8788 0246

Magnum's Wine Bar

10 Brewers Lane, TW9
☎020 8940 0427
Mon-Sat: 11am - 11pm
Sun: 11am - 10.30pm
18 @ £2.60 - £5.00
44 @ £9.95 - £85.00

Typically traditional

Tucked down a tiny lane off the main shopping street (look for a sandwich board sign on the pavement), Magnum's is the archetypal wine bar. Slightly chintzy, slightly quaint behind small-paned bowed windows, there is a long bar down one side and plenty of tables and chairs on the other. Faux-Parisian prints hang on pale yellow walls, with exposed brickwork to complete the effect. Wines encompass a comprehensive international selection, described on the list. The place has a friendly unpretentious atmosphere, ideal for passing shoppers or workers on the way home who don't wish to succumb to a bar chain or a fast-food outlet.

Paradise Winebar-Restaurant

1 Paradise Road, TW9
☎020 8332 7122
Mon-Fri: 8am - 11pm
Sat: Noon - 11pm; Sun: Noon - 10.30pm
11 @ £2.40 - £6.00
26 @ £8.90 - £45.00

Perfectly unpretentious

The corner location on the far side of the Richmond one-way giratory sounds unpromising, away from the bustle of the main shopping area. Yet the Paradise shows all the signs of being a popular local haunt, with amusingly-captioned photos of regular customers and friendly smiles as you walk in. A cheerful light-filled interior contains split-level seating areas, with green-tiled table tops. Daily papers are available for perusal, and lone customers are just as welcome as groups. The wine list contains established Old and New World names which will appeal to all palates and pockets.

⊖ ≷Richmond

The Red Room

14 Red Lion Street, TW9
☎020 8948 7300
Mon-Sat: 11am - 3pm/6pm - 11pm
10 @ £2.50 - £7.00
17 @ £10.50 - £35.00

"Anything as long as it's red"

The dark interior of this bijou bistro does indeed contain much of the eponymous colour, with swathes of draped material, mirrors down one wall, some comfortable seating and wrought iron tables and chairs lending a vaguely mediaeval air. The manager is anxious to create a chilled out atmosphere for customers, and his translation of the bistro concept is 'anything goes', in keeping with the colour theme. Luckily the wine list breaks the house rule and includes both white and sparkling bottles. The selection is at the whim of the manager, so if you can get into the groove of his laid-back approach, this could be the place for you.

Plus:

All Bar One
11 Hill Street, TW9
☎020 8332 7141

The Old Ship (Young's)
3 King Street, TW9
☎020 8940 3461

The Orange Tree (Young's)
45 Kew Road, TW9
☎020 8940 0944

Pitcher & Piano
11 Bridge Street, TW9
☎020 8332 2524

The Waterman's Arms (Young's)
12 Water Lane, TW9
☎020 8940 2893

The White Cross (Young's)
Riverside, TW9
☎020 8940 6844

Russell Square

Jacques Wine Bar

Tavistock Hotel, Tavistock Square, WC1
☎020 7636 8383 ext 8019
Mon-Sun: Noon - 11pm
14 @ £1.80 - £2.50 (125ml)
34 @ £8.00 - £35.50

Unique capital décor

There's nothing quite like the chrome, pink, green and grey design scheme inside Jacques, one of the house bars in the Tavistock Hotel. Geometric shapes and raised booths fill the bar which overlooks the square. Think '50s milkbar meets '80s designer and you're half way there! Don't let this put you off dropping in here for refreshment, especially if you've been in the British Museum nearby. There are very few other places locally which can beat Jacques for price and range (international, with thirteen French choices befitting the bar's name) in the wine stakes. And if you buy a bottle, they'll even let you drink it from 175ml glasses!

Vat's Wine Bar

51 Lamb's Conduit Street, WC1
☎020 7242 8963/020 7831 1611
Mon-Fri: Noon - 11pm
15 @ £3.25 - £5.95
90 @ £12.95 - £75.00

Wine-lovers' den

Off the beaten track but well-known to those who frequently make the trek from local offices or the Inns of Court, Vat's is the epitome of a London wine bar. Tardis-like inside, several cosy spaces run one into another ending in a bigger room at the back. It feels like stumbling into a house where everything is laid on for enjoying wine, with tables and chairs everywhere (even in the corridor between main rooms), an open fire in winter, and an extensive library of wine books for patrons to peruse. Local knowledge confirms that the bar snacks and nibbles are particularly good. Mein Host makes everybody welcome, and the wine list is a pleasure to read. There's an excellent range of French wines and a reasonable choice from other countries, perfect for washing down something hearty from the traditional British menu.

Plus:

The Calthorpe Arms (Young's)

252 Gray's Inn Road, WC1
☎020 7278 4732

The Lamb (Young's)

94 Lamb's Conduit Street, WC1
☎020 7405 0713

The Old Monk Exchange

61-71 Victoria Street, SW1
☎020 7233 2248
Mon-Fri: 11am - 11pm
9 @ £2.40 - £4.50
38 @ £9.95 - £45.90

Old habits die hard

This huge cellar wine bar in Strutton Ground has seen better days, but if you can get past the slightly rundown setting to take a look at the wine list you will be pleasantly surprised. Standard heavy wooden furniture and partitions fill the room, which has alcoves under arches where wines were formerly stored. The bar itself is sturdy, with wines racked up behind it. However it is the list which has all the interest: wines categorised by body rather than grape or region. On closer inspection, there is an Old and New World choice, with a further description, so it should not prove difficult to find something appealing. The presence of arcade machines and a distinctly old-school pub menu might be off-putting, but the wines deserve attention in spite of their surroundings.

Zander

45 Buckingham Gate, SW1
☎020 7379 9797
Mon-Sat: 6am - 11.30pm
Sun: 6am - 10pm
14 @ £3.20 - £7.00
76 @ £12.50 - £245.00

Long on designer chic

Attracting a reputation for taking the London bar scene onto another level, Zander boasts facilities for which most places would give their eye-teeth. The longest bar in Europe allows customers to stand or sit beside it for their drinks in relative comfort. Alternatively, sophisticated lighting, fashionably modern chairs, tables and banquettes provide luxurious accommodation for groups. Styled to within an inch of its life, Zander also maintains the cutting edge with its food and drink. Overall, the wines may be slightly more expensive than in similar establishments, but the choice is impressive and international. Beyond Zander at the back of the premises is Bank restaurant, where the same high standards continue.
www.bankrestaurants.com

Plus:

The Buckingham Arms (Young's)
62 Petty France, SW1
☎020 7222 3386

Tapster (Davy's)
3 Brewers' Green, Buckingham Gate, SW1
☎020 7222 0561

St John's Wood

The Duke of York Bar & Restaurant

2-2a St Ann's Terrace, NW8
☎020 7722 1933
Mon-Sat: 11am - 11pm
Sun: Noon - 10.30pm
11 @ £2.50 - £5.75
24 @ £10.25 - £38.00

Rock the Casbah

Despite the name, Moroccan influence permeates this corner bar, from metal lanterns to mosaic tabletops and iron grills on the windows. Colours are rich, and there is attention to detail in cushioned sofas and interesting wallhangings. The food menu is not as North African as the décor would suggest, although it looks tasty enough, and the wine list has only one Moroccan selection. The rest of it offers a balanced Old and New World selection. Essentially, this is a revamped pub, done with a modicum of imagination, and making a change from the rest of the area's dependency on bar chains.

The Salt House

63 Abbey Road, NW8
☎020 7328 6626
Mon-Sun: Noon - 11pm
20 @ £2.40 - £5.70
25 @ £9.95 - £60.00

All you need is wine

Pretend you're a Beatle as you negotiate the world's most famous zebra crossing, resist the temptation to scribble on the hallowed fence of the recording studios, then head north up Abbey Road until you reach the Salt House. Set on a leafy corner, it's pleasant to sit indoors or outside (depending on the weather) to make the most of the excellent food and wine available here. The wines on offer are written up on blackboards above the bar, with a mixed Old and New World selection which incorporates some unusual bottles not normally encountered on most lists. These include a Viognier, a Pinot Noir from Oregon, and a Priorato from eastern Spain. Worth investigating!

Plus:

All Bar One

60 St John's Wood High Street, NW8
☎020 7483 9931

49 Wine Bar

49 Gresham Street, EC2
020 7606 0399
Mon-Fri: Noon - 3pm
8 @ £2.60 - £3.15
16 @ £10.85 - £35.00

Cheerful choice

Downstairs at the corner of Wood Street, 49 is reached from street level by walking through the Fuller's pub above it. The cosy cellar bar is typical, with wood panelling and exposed brickwork, and walls lined with 18th and 19th century images of the City. A small bar/servery by the door dispenses hearty pub grub, and the wine list offers a standard selection boasting bottles from all the main international wine-producing countries. Everything about the bar is unruffled and relaxed, with prices to match, thus providing a welcome antidote to the hustle of the City outside.

Balls Brothers

6-8 Cheapside, EC2
020 7248 2708
Mon-Fri: 11.30am - 9.30pm
10 @ £3.30 - £4.50
82 @ £13.00 - £120.00

St Paul's local

This branch of the well-known wine bar chain deserves a mention for its location as much as for its excellent French and international wine selection. In a high-ceilinged old building at the back of St Paul's Cathedral, it makes a change not to have to go downstairs to enjoy the Balls Brothers treatment. On the contrary, tall windows let in plenty of natural light, but the real bonus is a circular paved area outside for summer drinking. From this vantage point you can watch the world go by, while admiring Sir Christopher Wren's masterpiece from a non-postcard angle. What would the saint make of it, as he looks back at the drinkers from his plinth in the churchyard opposite?
www.ballsbrothers.co.uk

The Old Monk

Corner Wood Street & Love Lane, EC2
020 7600 3500
Mon-Fri: 11am - 11pm
7 @ £2.40 - £3.60
19 @ £9.95 - £45.00

Count your blessings

Close to London Wall, the Old Monk looks out on an ancient tower standing sentinel in the shadow of modern high-rise development. The bar follows a tried-and-tested formula of providing the masses with food and drink in a relaxed lounge-style environment. With dark red walls, wood panelling, comfortable seating and interesting art installations, this is a cut above the standard chain bar, even if the food menu looks familiar. The wine list contains no real surprises, concentrating on well-known and widely available international brands. If all you want is a reliable (if unspectacular) drop to accompany lunch, or precede the journey home, the Old Monk could be what you're looking for.

Plus:

Balls Brothers

5-6 Carey Lane (off Gutter Lane), EC2
020 7600 2720

City Pipe (Davy's)

33 Foster Lane, EC2
020 7606 2110

Davy's at Russia Court

1-6 Milk Street, EC2
020 7600 2165

The Fine Line

1 Bow Churchyard, EC4
020 7248 3262

Albertine

1 Wood Lane, W12
020 8743 9593
Mon-Fri: 11am - 11pm
Sat: 6.30pm - 11pm
38 @ £2.50 - £4.40
100 @ £9.70 - £28.70

The real McCoy

One of the beauties of drinking wine in London is that you find treasures where you least expect them. Albertine is one of these, ploughing its own furrow for the last 30-odd years with a minimum of fuss and relying on good service, great food and fantastic wines to build its reputation. There couldn't be a greater contrast to the chaos of Shepherd's Bush outside. Albertine's interior is simple and comfortable, with wine memorabilia on the walls and bottles racked behind the small wooden bar. It's busy all day (packed at mealtimes) and is also ideal for a quiet drink at other times. The wine list cannot be praised highly enough – it definitely caters for all tastes, and provides plenty of opportunity for the daring to try something different.

The Havelock Tavern

57 Masbro Road, W14
020 7603 5374
Mon-Sat: 11am - 11pm
Sun: 11am - 10.30pm
10 @ £2.40 - £4.00
27 @ £9.50 - £25.00

Lucky locals

Out of the way down quiet streets beyond Brook Green, the Havelock is a revelation. This is a comfortable old pub which has been through the inevitable modernising yet still managed to retain its charm. It has a '20s-style tiled exterior, a huge rectangular bar in pride of place in the centre of the room, huge windows and even a small courtyard at the back. The international wine list changes reasonably regularly and is chalked up on blackboards (as is the food menu which changes daily for lunch and dinner). If this was your local it would be hard to walk past, and it's certainly worth trekking up here from the Tube.

Sloane Square

The Front Page

35 Old Church Street, Chelsea, SW10
☎020 7352 6465
Mon-Sat: 11am - 11pm
Sun: Noon - 10.30pm
9 @ £2.60 - £7.50
30 @ £11.00 - £55.00

Stop press!

This is your reward for braving the King's Road all the way from the Tube station. If you can't wait, jump on a No.11 bus and get off when you see the cinema on the left. It's on the corner of Paulton Street, opposite a quaint old dairy which has sculpted cows' heads emerging from the façade. This alone is worth the trek! The pub itself is cosy and relaxed, fitting in well with the ever-so-respectable residential area outside. Think civilised gents' club rather than beer barn. Wines are international and represent good value, with descriptions given on the list. The Sporting Page in Camera Place on the Fulham side of the King's Road is also part of this London-wide mini-chain.
www.frontpagepubs.com

Oriel

50-51 Sloane Square, SW1
☎020 7730 2804
Mon-Sat: 8.30am - 10.45pm
Sun: 9am - 10.30pm
19 @ £3.00 - £5.60
30 @ £12.15 - £57.80

More French than France itself

You could be forgiven for thinking you were in central Paris on entering this fabulous mirrored salon on Sloane Square near the Royal Court Theatre. This is glamour writ large, from substantial bar to ornate light fittings via marble, gilt and mosaics. There is al fresco pavement seating for dedicated people-watchers, and downstairs lies a less formal room with sofas and further tables. In true brasserie style, the menu is eclectic and covers all possible food and drink requirements. The wine list (no vintages given) is predominantly French, though some New World bottles have also made the grade. Oriel's smartly-dressed clientele ranges from grandes dames to designer-clad youth, and it's always busy, attesting to its reputation for style and service.

Plus:

Pitcher & Piano

316-318 King's Road, SW3
☎020 7352 0025

The Rising Sun (Young's)

46 Ebury Bridge Road, SW1
☎020 7730 4088

The Builder's Arms

13 Britten Street, SW3
020 7349 9040
Mon-Sat: 11am - 11pm
Sun: Noon - 10.30pm
10 @ £2.50 - £5.00
28 @ £9.50 - £42.00

Leafy gastropub

Not far off the King's Road, the Builder's Arms makes an ideal retreat for those who have no interest in shopping, or for those who have shopped too much (if that is conceivable). The bar creates a central divider between a smart pub-style zone on one side and a living room/library themed space on the other. This is refined gastropub territory, reflecting the genteel Chelsea neighbourhood outside. The wine list follows international lines, and unusually, goes from most expensive to cheapest. There are quality brands represented, as well as bin ends and special interest wines on a separate list. If pubs are your thing, but you fancy a decent glass of wine, the Builder's Arms could be the place for you.

The Crescent

99 Fulham Road, SW3
020 7225 2244
Mon: 11am - 11pm
Tue-Sat: 10am - 11pm; Sun: 11am - 10.30pm
21 @ £2.75 - £8.50
154 @ £9.95 - £115.00

Wine for the 21st century

If wine bars were evolving organisms, The Crescent is what '70s/'80s specimens might well have become in response to the changing environment around them. Here is a clean-lined, modern bar, with a small room at street level and a larger space below stairs, minimalist but not aggressively so – and with wines to die for. Having a respected wine writer at the helm helps, but you don't need to be an expert to enjoy the riches available here. The list is extensive, half French and half Old and New World, including a wine for every pocket and some genuine treats. In addition, The Crescent holds regular tutored tasting events for those wishing to develop their palate. Wine-lovers' heaven.

PJ's Bar & Grill

52 Fulham Road, SW3
020 7581 0025
Mon-Sat: Noon - Midnight
Sun: Noon - 10.30pm
15 @ £3.45 - £6.95
48 @ £11.95 - £110.00

Club casual

Stroll into PJ's and the first thing that strikes you is its resemblance to a colonial club, with ancient mirror and wood panelling, an overhead fan and old photos of polo and rowing teams. Above the highly-polished central bar an aeroplane propeller and engine are suspended, bringing to mind swashbuckling tales of bravado à la Ernest Hemingway. So much for setting the scene for the well-heeled clientele who flock here from the nearby shops of Kensington and Chelsea. Staff are friendly and efficient, and will bring you your choice from an international wine list which abounds in well-known names. This may not be adventurous, but reliability never goes amiss.

Plus:

All Bar One
311-313 Fulham Road, SW10
020 7349 1751

Finch's (Young's)
190 Fulham Road, SW10
020 7351 5043

The Fine Line
236 Fulham Road, SW10
020 7376 5827

Pitcher & Piano
214 Fulham Road, SW10
020 7352 9234

Bar Citrus

36 The Cut, SE1
☎020 7633 9144
Mon-Sat: 11am - 11pm
Sun: Noon - 10.30pm
19 @ £2.10 - £3.35
19 @ £8.25 - £12.75

Pithy selection

On a corner near the Young Vic theatre, Bar Citrus ressembles other places of its ilk – pale wood, a random assortment of wooden tables and chairs, French windows which open wide onto the street in good weather, the kitchen visible in one corner. Where it differs is in a reasonably-priced list of wines by both glass and bottle, generally a white and a red from each of the better-known world wine countries. Don't come here to find top of the range product, but for pleasant quaffing wine to be enjoyed in relaxed surroundings, Bar Citrus definitely fits the bill. For non-wine drinkers, the full range of pub and café drink choices is appreciated too.
www.barcitrus.co.uk

Blackfriars Pavilion

242 Blackfriars Road, SE1
☎020 7928 8689
Mon-Fri: 11.30am - 8.30pm
8 @ £2.50 - £4.60
62 @ £9.45 - £42.50

Business as usual

Also known simply as 242, the Pavilion's entrance is under railway arches at the top of a cobbled ramp by the junction of Blackfriars Road and Southwark Street. Down a spiral staircase, the interior has a slightly dated feel, with plenty of chrome and leatherette. However the wine list is up to the minute, handily divided into quaffing and fine wines, with French classics alongside respectable international representation. Primarily a business haunt at lunchtime, the distance between the bar and local offices (north and south of the river) is ideal for a restorative post-prandial stroll. One customer confided that the Pavilion rated "10/10 for service". Events such as an annual golf tournament show that this is a bar which likes to take care of its clientele beyond the feeding and watering which is its stock in trade.

Southwark

Blackfriars Wine Bar

Arch 80, Scoresby Street, SE1
☎020 7928 0905
Mon-Fri: 11am - 9pm
7 @ 2.30 - £4.50
57 @ £8.50 - £35.00

Traditional style and value

This wine bar sits in one of the railway arches at the far end of the street, a short walk from the Tube station. Doubling as a wine warehouse, large wooden barrels outside indicate that you are heading in the right direction for a friendly welcome and a well-priced wine selection. Inside, conversation is punctuated by the occasional noise of a train, but this just adds to the character of the place. Owner/manager Terry, full of bonhomie, has ready banter for locals and newcomers alike. The food is hearty, ideal for accompanying one of the many bottles available from France and elsewhere. The bar runs a series of wine appreciation courses too, for those who want to develop their knowledge and palate.
www.blackfriarswinebar.co.uk

Meson Don Felipe

53 The Cut, SE1
☎020 7928 3237
Mon-Sat: Noon - 11pm
18 @ £2.45 - £3.95
87 @ £9.95 - £65.00

Spanish specialists south of the river

A rather foreboding exterior of dark brick, green awnings and barred high windows opposite the Young Vic theatre is initially off-putting, but don't be fooled. Behind the heavy wooden door lies a revelation. A rectangular wooden bar fills the centre of a pink room, surrounded by tables and chairs which are snapped up by those who are already aficionados of the bar. A curious collection of Hispano-English memorabilia covers the walls: Iberian tiles, cricket rules and gear, Spanish plates and mirrors. Delicious tapas are available to accompany wines from a list that covers most Spanish regions, and includes several sherries. Everything about the place screams authenticity, and if you're quick enough to get a table, you won't be going far for the rest of the night.

Plus:

The Founder's Arms (Young's)

52 Hopton Street, SE1
☎020 7928 1899

Café Med

320 Goldhawk Road, W6
☎020 8741 1994
Mon-Sat: Noon - 11pm
Sun: Noon - 10.30pm
13 @ £2.75 - £6.25
37 @ £9.95 - £42.00

Magical mystery tour

Head north from the Tube and keep walking. Just when you think you are going in the wrong direction and Goldhawk Road station would be closer (it's not), Chiswick's version of the Café Med mini-chain appears. Reward yourself without stinting, for here you will find an old-fashioned pub transformed into comfortable luxury, with food and drink to match. Dining on the left of the door and drinking on the right, an open fire, a grand piano, dark wood and clever skylighting, leather sofas in mad colours, plus a courtyard at the back for sunny days: all this offers an environment for every occasion. Wines are international, with some interesting grape varieties as well as the standards. This couldn't feel any less like a chain, so make the most of it!

Casa

30-34 Chiswick High Road, W4
☎020 8742 0021
Mon-Sat: 11am - 11pm
Sun: 11am - 10.30pm
15 @ £2.50 - £3.60
17 @ £9.50 - £80.00

Young and lively

Another player joining the burgeoning bar chain scene across London, Casa appeals to the young evening crowd out for fun and good times. Here in Chiswick the bar fills a huge space, with three distinct areas: a raised table-seating section by the big street-front windows, comfortable sofas near the door, and a fireplace zone at the back under a skylight. The long curved bar is designed for serving as many people as possible, so the overall level of sophistication is not high. However if you want to drink wine here, you will find a small but reasonable international selection which includes a couple of organic options.

Stamford Brook

The Hart (bar room bar)

383 King Street, W4
☎020 8748 6076
Mon-Thu: 11am - 11pm
Fri & Sat: 11am - Midnight; Sun: 11am - 10.30pm
11 @ £2.50 - £3.65
16 @ £10.00 - £50.00

Home away from home

The Hart has elements of everybody's ideal living room: weathered tables and chairs to rugs on the floor, sofas and armchairs, table football and a snooker table, French windows opening out onto a garden at the back, and best of all, plenty of space. The neutrally-coloured walls are decorated with regularly-changing art exhibitions. In keeping with the populist theme, food and drink cover all possible preferences. Wines are cheap and cheerful international choices, well-suited to the relaxed atmosphere of the bar. This successful formula is repeated elsewhere in London, so if you see the tell-tale "brb" initials appended to a bar name, you will know what to expect.

Plus:

Pitcher & Piano

18-20 Chiswick High Road, W4
☎020 8742 7731

Swiss Cottage

The Arches ⇌

7 Fairhazel Gardens, NW6
☎020 7624 1867
Mon-Sat: Noon - Midnight
Sun: Noon - 11pm
11 @ £2.50 - £5.00
63 @ £9.95 - £75.00

True original

Named after the arches in the old song, the owner of this former Victorian bakery turned bric-a-brac shop turned wine bar possesses the original Westminster street sign, along with an incredible array of other artefacts and curiosities. Matching this collection for diversity and interest, and beyond the permanently-listed wines, there are a further 140+ bottles and bin ends from all over the world. Customers are invited to appreciate and enjoy, safe in the knowledge that they can try some real treats and not be ripped off on price. Staff can recommend wines, and it's also possible to sample a glass of something from the bottle menu. Chances are you'll like it so much that drinking the rest of the bottle won't present any difficulty. With nothing else like it anywhere in London, this place has to be experienced at least once in a lifetime's wine-loving.

Plus:

Café Med ⇌

21 Loudoun Road, NW8
☎020 7625 1222

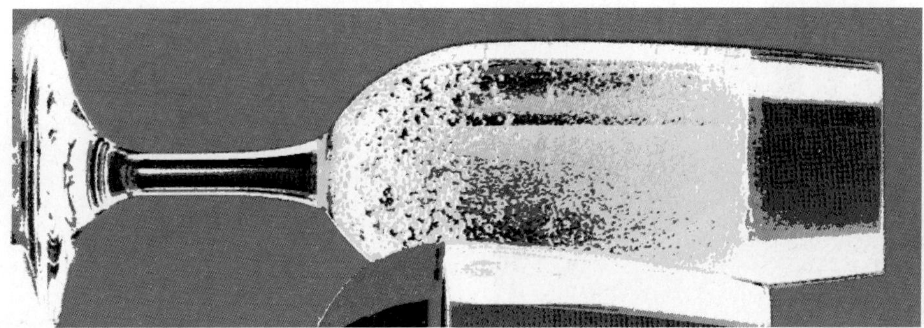

⊖ Temple

Columbia Bar ⊖

69 Aldwych, WC2
☎020 7831 8043
Mon-Thu: 10am - 11pm
Fri: 10am - 1am
28 @ £2.75 - £5.00
35 @ £11.85 - £45.00

Justice is done

Nestled on the curve of Aldwych on the way to the Royal Courts of Justice, the Columbia is another of the Young's Brewery forays into upmarket bar territory. This venue would not be out of place in downtown Manhattan, with tall windows and chrome details creating a smart-casual interior. Autumnal furniture tones and unobtrusive wall-prints provide a restful place for a drink, but by the same token, the Columbia hops at busy times of day. The Young's connection ensures a well-kept and varied international wine selection which will appeal to all palates, as well as cater for all price brackets.

Daly's Wine Bar

210 Strand, WC2
☎020 7583 4476
Mon-Fri: 10am - 11pm
14 @ £2.60 - £4.50
53 @ £9.95 - £109.95

Judicious selection

Opposite the Royal Courts of Justice at the kink in the road where the Strand becomes Fleet Street, Daly's has the feel of an old London inn, with small-paned windows, cosy booths and plenty of standing room by the solid wooden bar. Inevitably barristers and their clients are drawn here for Dutch courage or congratulatory drinks; there are probably more briefcases per square metre in Daly's than anywhere else in London. After office hours they are joined by other professionals in search of a civilised drink or two. The wine list rounds up all the usual suspects without indulging in daylight robbery, and a range of Champagnes is kept on ice for those who have something to celebrate.

El Vino ⊖

47 Fleet Street, EC4
☎020 7353 6786
Mon-Fri: 8.30am - 11pm
20 @ £2.90 - £6.20 (125ml)
150+@ £11.50 - £185.00

Masters of wine

One of four El Vino outlets in the City, this Fleet Street venue is recognised as the inspiration for the watering hole in John Mortimer's "Rumpole of the Bailey" books. A wine bar of the old school, the room is all cosy wood and leather, with antique gadgets and black-and-white photos of yesteryear lurking in every nook and cranny. El Vino's alternative rôle as a wine merchant ensures a comprehensive international wine list, and staff are able to make recommendations if the selection proves to be overwhelming. El Vino also offers tutored wine tastings and a mail order wine service, making it into a one-stop shop for everything a wine-lover could possibly require.

The Wine Press ⊖

161 Fleet Street, EC4
☎020 7353 9550
Mon-Fri: 11.30am - 11.30pm
20 @ £3.00 - £3.95
50 @ £9.50 - £80.00

Enjoy the crush

A real find, unless you work in the area, in which case you will already be familiar with this venue's relaxed style. An unprepossessing exterior on the north side of Fleet Street belies the lively atmosphere to be found within. Tables are set up cheek-by-jowl in a large room, with a raised bar area at the front. There is a distinctly continental feel to the premises, an impression which is enhanced by red gingham tablecloths and a predominantly Italian menu. The wine list is international, and although it doesn't have as wide an Italian selection as the food choice would suggest, it represents good value for money. Clearly the local workers know this, as it's always busy, no matter what time of day or night.

The Couch

97-99 Dean Street, Soho, W1
☎020 7287 0150
Mon-Fri: 9.30am - 11pm
Sat: 11am - 11pm; Sun: Noon - 10.30pm
25 @ £2.90 - £8.00
29 @ £10.50 - £50.00

"Eat well, drink lots and couch out"

Such is the legend hanging outside this comfortable modernised pub on the Oxford Street side of Soho. Indeed, all these activities are possible inside a large well-appointed room, which has big windows along the front, and caters for people who wish to sit up at tables and chairs or sink back into sofas and armchairs. An ornate bar and electric chandeliers hark back to the former establishment, but food and drinks are thoroughly modern. Wines have been sourced from all over the world, and although there are no surprises, they are reasonably priced and available in several measures. Being so close to one of the capital's main shopping districts, The Couch is a pleasant antidote to both the crowds and the fast-food outlets prevalent in the area.

Freud's Café Bar

198 Shaftesbury Avenue, WC2
☎020 7240 9933
Mon-Sat: 11am - 11pm
Sun: Noon - 10.30pm
2 @ £1.75 (125ml)
10 @ £9.95 - £31.95

Exception to the rule

Given the minimal nature of the wine list, Freud's wouldn't usually make it into this guide. However, we can always make room for style. Down some fairly precipitous metal steps underneath the Freud shop at the top end of Shaftesbury Avenue, the bar is a textured temple of cool. A wide leather banquette runs around the edges of the stone room, which seems to have been carved out of the cellar space. Art exhibits change monthly. Although the wines on offer are few, they have been well-chosen. Freud's is worth knowing about if one of the local pubs holds no appeal for a pre-theatre drink or two.

Tottenham Court Road

Grape Street Wine Bar

224a Shaftesbury Avenue, WC2
☎020 7240 0686
Mon-Fri: 11am - 11pm
16 @ £2.50 - £5.50
50 @ £9.95 - £70.00

Aladdin's cave of wine

This is a great find right at the top of Shaftesbury Avenue. In many ways it's typical, being in a downstairs room with various alcoves and slightly dated décor. Yet in attention to detail, Grape Street stands out from the crowd. The wines themselves cover an excellent, well-priced range of French and New World bottles, presented in a list which finishes with quotes about wine. The inevitable wine posters and old bottles may appear familiar, but look more closely and you will discover some classics. The highlight of Grape Street, though, is the reading material available. For the wine connoisseur, back copies of "Decanter" and other trade magazines are provided. Those who prefer fiction are invited to borrow from the Grape Street library of paperbacks, on the stairs by the entrance. Truly civilised.

Jerusalem

33-34 Rathbone Place, W1
☎020 7255 1120
Mon-Fri: Noon - 11pm
Sat: 7pm - 11pm
8 @ £2.80 - £6.00
25 @ £11.00 - £100.00

Join the Crusades

My Mum used to tell me that "Patience and perseverance took snails to Jerusalem", and you will need both qualities to locate this unusual bar. It's down some metal stairs at the north end of Rathbone Place, not particularly well-signposted in daylight. There is nothing else quite like it in mainstream London. Mediaeval effects abound, from heavy velvet curtains to candles inside wrought-iron globes on heavy tables which look like they have come straight from Richard the Lionheart's banqueting hall. Fetch one of the impressive selection of international wines from the wide concrete bar, order some food, and let your imagination run wild. Wines change every six to eight weeks, and the management awaits the outcome of a late licence application.

Tottenham Court Road

The Phoenix Artist Club

I Phoenix Street, Charing Cross Road, WC2
☎020 7836 1077
Mon-Wed: 5pm - 2am
Thu-Sat: 12.30pm - 3am
5 @ £2.60 - £2.70 (125ml)
20 @ £8.95 - £29.95

It's showtime!

The late licence operates for members, but earlier in the evening anyone will be welcome into this dramatic basement cavern. More or less opposite Foyle's bookshop, the Phoenix is underneath the theatre of the same name. Dark, smoky, filled with nostalgic theatrical memorabilia and props, the club ressembles a museum as much as a drinking den for artistes. It was in the theatre that Laurence Olivier made his London début in 1930. It's worth going to the Phoenix at least once in your life if you have a passing interest in things thespian. Wines are regulation issue international, but you're here for the atmosphere more than anything else.

Plus:

All Bar One

108 New Oxford Street, WC1
☎020 7307 7980

Chez Gérard

8 Charlotte Street, W1
☎020 7636 4975

Tower Hill

The Aquarium Bang Bar

St Katharine's Dock, E1
☎020 7480 6116
Mon-Fri: Noon - 11pm
Sat: 4pm - 11pm
13 @ £3.00 - £5.50
18 @ £10.50 - £165.00

Maritime haven

This is a simple bar above the fabulous Aquarium restaurant, overlooking stunning St Katharine's Dock which is crammed full of expensive ocean-going vessels. It's an ideal spot for summer quaffing, located within a converted warehouse and full of comfortable sofas, with big windows open above the sparkling water. The wine list is reasonably short but covers the basics well from both the New and Old Worlds. The Bang Bar is the place to escape to for a simple glass of quality wine amidst the opulence of this metropolitan marina.

www.theaquarium.co.uk

Chuzzlewit's Wine Bar & Restaurant

Cardinal Court, 21 St Thomas More Street, E1
☎020 7709 9191
Mon-Fri: 8.30am - 11pm
22 @ £2.75 - £6.00
49 @ £10.95 - £48.95

Calm sophistication

Set below the towering office blocks of St Thomas More Street and a stone's throw from St Katharine's Dock, Chuzzlewits offers its customers a bright, modern and efficient bar-restaurant, serving delicious food and a very solid selection of wines. The terrace has tables and chairs set outside for those occasional summer days. Wines offered here are divided intelligently under headings such as "light and crisp" and "generous and oaky" for whites, and "medium-bodied" and "rich, spicy and firm" for reds. The list is reasonably long, with some interesting examples of less common grapes such as Primitivo, Viognier, Malvasia and Pinot Blanc amongst more classic wines from Europe and the New World. A treat for residents and workers in this part of town.

Docks Bar & Diner

66a Royal Mint Street, E1
020 7488 4144
Mon-Wed: 11am - 8.30pm
Thurs & Fri: 11am - 11pm
12 @ £2.95 - £5.35
24 @ £11.75 - £45.50

Davy's with a difference

Perched on a fairly unsalubrious corner in this part of East London not far from Tower Hill is this Davy's bar which is untypical of the chain. The bar is large with wooden floors, painted bright yellow and blue, with a large TV screen taking up an entire wall. The welcome is friendly however, though the wine list is shorter and less diverse than that on offer in the majority of Davy's bars. This list is full of Davy's own branded classics with only a few named producers creeping in at the edges. Safe and sound for anyone in the area after a reliable glass of wine. Live jazz on Fridays.
www.davy.co.uk

The Emperor Wine Bar

35 Vine Street, EC3
020 7481 2885
Mon-Fri: 11.30am - 10pm
11 @ £2.70 - £3.25
53 @ £10.50 - £47.50

Little Italy

Hidden away in a quiet street amongst the office blocks of Vine Street, the Emperor wine bar is a firm favourite of those who are employed by the banks and the law firms in the vicinity. Its spacious interior allows plenty of room for each table, with alcoves dotted about, and the Italian staff are pleasant and friendly. The wine list is heavily weighted in favour of the fine wines of Italy, but it also offers classics from the rest of Europe. If you want a decent choice of regional wines, this is a handy place to know about.

Tower Hill

The Wine Library

43 Trinity Square, EC3
020 7481 0415
Wine Merchant: Mon-Sun: 10am - 6pm
Lunch served: Mon-Fri: 11am - 3pm
None listed
from £5.85

Unique edition

Tucked away down a narrow staircase at one end of fabulous Trinity Square is the Wine Library. Push open the door and enter a vinous Aladdin's cave. The Wine Library is a fine wine merchant with all its wares on display, crammed onto 'bookshelves' dominating the tiny interior. Everything is here, from top crus classés Bordeaux, Penfold's Grange, major US vineyards and Burgundies, to a wide variety of lesser known and more affordable international choices. Wine books and magazines adorn shelves at the far end and serve to concentrate the hushed atmosphere, so conducive to awe-inspired browsing. Buffet lunch is offered in an adjoining room for £11.95, and wines may be selected from the library at the shop price plus a small corkage fee. (Booking in advance is essential for lunch, due to limited space.) Ports and dessert wines are available by the glass. Don't miss it!

Plus:

All Bar One
16 Byward Street, EC3
020 7553 0301

Balls Brothers
Mark Lane, EC3
020 7623 2923

Chez Gérard
14 Trinity Square, EC3
020 7480 5500

The Fine Line
124-127 The Minories, EC3
020 7481 8195

The Habit & New Waterloo (Davy's)
Friary Court, 65 Crutched Friars, EC3
020 7283 1131

Jamies
119-121 The Minories, EC3
020 7709 9900

The Vineyard (Davy's)
International house, 1 St Katharine's Way, E1
020 7480 6680

The Dartmouth Arms
35 York Rise, NW5
020 7485 3267
Mon-Sat: 11am - 11pm
Sun: 10am - 10.30pm
6 @ £2.50 - £2.75
19 @ £8.95 - £36.00

Don't be deceived

It would be so easy to walk past the Dartmouth Arms, not because it's difficult to locate, but because from the street it looks more like a rather smoky local than a gastropub which merits closer inspection. In fact, two comfortable rooms inside are home to the kind of welcome which makes you want to return, especially after gaining a full appreciation of the range of food and drink served here. The inexpensive wines are mostly from the Old World, but there are plans to expand the list, and the management organises tasting events from time to time. The Dartmouth combines all the positive points of a neighbourhood pub with the ambition of a more sophisticated enterprise, and gets the blend just right.

Lord Palmerston
33 Dartmouth Park Hill, NW5
020 7485 1578
Mon-Sat: Noon - 11pm
Sun: Noon - 10.30pm
21 @ £2.40 - £4.40
25 @ £8.70 - £22.00

Refreshing approach

On the corner of Chetwynd Road, the Lord Palmerston's light and airy premises are home to one of the best gastropub wine selections you are likely to find in London. Operating on the principle that there will always be a certain number of wines available, rather than specific bottles, the owner is able to make tactical substitutions when he finds something he likes and wants to share. The benefit of this for customers is an impressive international selection which includes big name producers as well as delicious curiosities. These are chalked up on boards in the main bar area, and it's an added bonus that the majority are sold by the glass.

Gravy Bar & Restaurant

142 Chiswick High Road, W4
020 8994 6816
Mon-Fri: Noon - 4pm/5.30pm - 11pm
Sat: 8.30am - 4pm/5.30pm - 11pm
Sun: Noon - 11pm
16 @ £2.20 - £5.00
46 @ £10.50 - £65.00

Originality and style

A welcome addition to the Chiswick scene, which otherwise tends to be dominated by bar chains and café-brasseries, Gravy actively encourages casual drinkers as well as diners. Whether indoors at the long banquette running down the side wall, or under the dark red awning at one of the pavement tables, ultra-friendly staff will look after you royally. The wine list is based on the owner's preferences, but he has good taste and you should not be deterred from an eclectic yet accessible range. You won't find many places in this area with such an interesting and varied choice, or such well-appointed design in which to enjoy the wine.

The Paragon

80-82 Chiswick High Road, W4
020 8742 7263
Mon-Sat: Noon - 11pm
Sun: Noon - 10.30pm
12 @ £2.45 - £2.75
16 @ £10.25 - £30.00

A step up from publand

The Air Force blue of the exterior paintwork on the Paragon signals its inclusion in the expanding Smith & Jones/Barracuda pub empire – there are similar examples all over London with the same colouring and sign-writing. Inside is a fairly typical upmarket take on a standard pub, with tables and chairs of all descriptions, a few sofas and even a piano. Wines are mostly from the New World, but to find any pub which offers more than Château Box Red, or white wine from one of those wall-hanging coolers, is a mighty relief. The Paragon doesn't quite make it into true gastropub territory, but it does the basics effectively and deserves credit for that.

Pug

68 Chiswick High Road, W4
020 8987 9988
Mon-Sat: 11am - 11pm
Sun: 11am - 10.30pm
11 @ £2.85 - £6.00
36 @ £11.95 - £45.00

Cool, calm and collected

Set back from the busy road, Pug benefits from plenty of space in which to spread out its different functions of bar, lounge and restaurant. There's even a sheltered courtyard by the entrance for sitting out in fine weather. The elegantly-styled interior boasts quiet booths, comfortable sofas and pouffes, and a formal dining area separated from the main bar by a glass screen. With the restaurant adjacent, Pug can offer casual drinkers an excellent selection of wines, international in origin and covering an interesting range of grapes and styles. Pug represents cosmopolitan class out West – who needs the hassle of the journey into town when this is on the doorstep?

Plus:

All Bar One
197-199 Chiswick High Road, W4
020 8987 8211

Crown and Anchor (Young's)
374 Chiswick High Road, W4
020 8995 2607

Twickenham

Osteria Pulcinella

36 Church Street, Twickenham, TW1
020 8892 5854
Mon-Sat: 9.30am - 11pm
Sun: 9.30am - 10.30pm
10 @ £2.75 - £5.75
34 @ £9.50 - £49.50

Italian all the way

Twickenham is largely restaurant land, or else sports bars for the rugby crowds on match days. Yet occasionally you come across an exception to the rule. Osteria Pulcinella is down a small lane off the main road, and concentrates mainly on lunch and dinner, but wine-lovers are welcome for drinks only too. The pleasantly rustic style includes a bar built on the top of vertically split wine barrels. An exclusively Italian wine list complements traditional food. Osteria Pulcinella aims to cover many bases with its café-bar-restaurant remit, and succeeds on all of them, with a healthy dose of laid-back charm for good measure.

Plus:

All Bar One

26-28 York Road, TW1
020 8843 7281

Pope's Grotto (Young's)

Cross Deep, TW1
020 8892 3050

Vauxhall

Bar Estrela

111-115 South Lambeth Road, SW8
020 7793 1051
Mon-Sat: 8am - Midnight
Sun: 11am - 9pm
None listed
28 @ £7.50 - £35.00

Portuguese, pure and simple

This pocket of the capital is Portuguese through and through, with a plethora of cafes and restaurants dealing in Lusitanian specialities. For wine without the obligation to order a three-course meal, Bar Estrela is the best of the bunch, although it does a tasty food selection for those with an appetite. Apart from some token Champagne, the wine list here is exclusively Portuguese, with four Vinhos Verdes given special attention. None is available by the glass, but then again, none of the bottles is too expensive so two people sharing is very economical. The bar occupies a tiled room decorated with framed posters of the old country, and the chrome counter rests above glass cabinets displaying some of the snacks. If Portugal is your passion but the holidays are still too far away, make South Lambeth your destination!

Carriages

43 Buckingham Palace Road, SW1
☎020 7834 0119
Mon-Fri: Noon - 11pm
27 @ £3.10 - £5.00
62 @ £11.50 - £44.00

Popular with parties

Walking towards Buckingham Palace from Victoria station, Carriages' blue-painted front and big windows appear on the left side of the road. A small bar area at the front of the room quickly becomes tabled seating, with potted plants to break up the spacious room. The venue is clearly popular with local workers, and is particularly suitable for groups, as the atmosphere generated is bustling and informal. The international wine list is extensive and caters for all tastes, listed here by "body" rather than country or grape. For a crowd of friends out for a good night's eating and drinking, Carriages offers something for everyone.

Ebury Wine Bar & Restaurant

139 Elizabeth Street, SW1
☎020 7730 5447
Mon-Sat: Noon - 11pm
Sun: 6pm - 10pm
27 @ £3.10 - £5.00
62 @ £11.50 - £44.00

Pretty as a picture

The façade of the Ebury blends in perfectly with the neighbouring shops in well-heeled Belgravia: flowering plants, an awning, black-painted railings and small-paned windows. Inside, the chocolate box effect is continued with rural scenes painted directly onto the walls. Risqué prints of Parisians kicking up their heels prove that the Ebury has a welcome sense of humour too. There is a small bar area at the front, with a rather incongruous large screen TV in one corner, with the restaurant at the rear. The wines on offer cover a broad international selection and are listed by "body" rather than grape variety. They are priced reasonably enough for you to go shopping afterwards in Elizabeth Street and still contemplate a small purchase.

Justin de Blank

50-52 Buckingham Palace Road, SW1
☎020 7828 4111
Mon-Fri: 11am - 11pm
16 @ £2.55 - £5.20
39 @ £9.90 - £150.00

Perfect for people-watching

This brasserie-restaurant looks unpromisingly tacky from the outside, with blacked out windows covered in busy writing. Go in the corner-located front door to the bar however, and discover a light high-ceilinged interior – and realise immediately that you can watch the passersby but they can't see you. That blackness has its purpose! Sofas, high and low tables, and plenty of standing room give several options when meeting friends for drinks after work; if you want a touch more civilisation, go through to the restaurant, although you will need to eat to guarantee a seat. Pavement tables are available when it's fine. The wine list is mainly French, with New World offerings for variety. All of which proves that you can't judge a book by its cover – step inside Justin de Blank and be ready for a pleasant surprise.

Tiles Restaurant & Bar

36 Buckingham Palace Road, SW1
☎020 7834 7761
Mon-Fri: 11am - 11pm
16 @ £2.50 - £6.50
47 @ £9.95 - £43.00

Quiet haven near Queen's house

Red paintwork around big picture windows reveals dining tables and chairs inside Tiles, but don't be fooled: there is a bijou bar at the back of the room, and people drop in for drinks just as much as to enjoy the affordable menu. The wines are fully described on the wide-ranging international list, and there are specials available too. Very close to the busy station, Tiles is perfect for a relaxed drink over lunch or on the way home from work. It also has the attributes for an intimate rendez-vous if you are looking for a romantic venue which won't frighten the horses.

Vino Veritas

44 Elizabeth Street, SW1
☎020 7730 5437
Mon-Fri: 11am - 11pm
10 @ £2.50 - £3.25
11 @ £9.55 - £13.10

Plain truth

A salubrious location amongst the specialist shops of Elizabeth Street indicates serious quaffing opportunities – but, despite the sign over the door, this is more pub than dedicated wine emporium. For all that, the limited list is international, and with most of it available by glass, a quick drink here in between boutiques holds some appeal. The space is divided into two distinct areas, warm comfortable bar at the front with wine quotes painted on the walls, and dining at the rear. Other wine bric-a-brac continues the vinous theme, but be prepared to see as many pints as wine glasses if you drop in for refreshments.

Plus:

The Reef

Victoria Station Concourse, SW1
☎020 7834 4387

Henry's Café and Bar

14 Balkan Walk, Tobacco Dock, E1
☎020 7379 1871
Mon-Thurs: Noon - 8pm
Fri: Noon - 11pm
20 @ £2.40 - £5.95
22 @ £9.25 - £80.00

Splendid isolation

This Henry's bar has been in Tobacco Dock for some years, but is the only surviving outlet in this ghost of a retail complex. The bar has a lovely tropical ambience amidst wicker furniture and hundreds of large indoor plants under glorious timber beams. The old cutter sailing ships in dry dock in front of the bar are unfortunately under scaffolding at the time of writing, but this is still a very pleasant setting in the middle of Wapping by the canal. Henry's offers a reasonable selection of classic wines by the glass and the bottle, along with hearty fare, and those seeking a reliable quaff in pleasant surrounds will not go far wrong here.

⊖ ⇄Waterloo (East)

The Archduke

Concert Hall Approach, South Bank, SE1
☎020 7928 9370
Mon-Fri: 8.30am - 11pm
Sat: 11am - 11pm
10 @ £2.65 - £3.55
33 @ £10.50 - £39.50

Wine, jazz, coffee – a winning combo

As you approach the Royal Festival Hall from Waterloo, keep your ears open for the strains of jazz emanating from railway arches on your left. Follow the sound into an attractive brick-lined space with seating on different levels, food for all appetites, and a wine list which covers Old and New World tastes. Piped or live jazz overcomes the percussive rumble of trains overhead, making this place the ideal prelude to a concert or an exhibition in the nearby South Bank complex. Popular with musicians between afternoon rehearsal and evening performance, rumour has it that those who are 'resting' also turn up here with their instruments, thereby creating an aura of being in demand.

Azzurro

Sutton Walk, SE1
☎020 7620 1300
Mon-Sat: 11am - 11pm
Sun: Noon - 10.30pm
11 @ £2.35 - £3.95
12 @ £9.95 - £34.95

Mainly Italian mini-selection

Underneath a bridge arch diagonally opposite the main entrance to Waterloo railway station is perhaps the last place you would expect to find an Italian trattoria. Yet here it is – in a modern style, with cool flagstone floors and chunky wooden furniture sitting well in the Victorian brickwork. Glass fills the arch, letting in plenty of light, and affording a view of the commuters scurrying to and fro outside. A staircase at the back of the spacious bar area takes you up to the dining section. The majority of the wines are Italian, nothing flash, but perfectly acceptable on their own or with pizza or pasta. As an alternative to what's on offer in the station, or other local options, Azzurro is a welcome addition to the Waterloo landscape.

The Fire Station

150 Waterloo Road, SE1
☎020 7620 2226
Mon-Sat: 11am - 11pm
Sun: 11am - 10.30pm
11 @ £2.45 - £5.60
41 @ £10.25 - £42.50

Raise the alarm!

A popular venue with a varied clientele, the Fire Station presents a microcosm of big city life. Depending on when you are in this cavernous tiled space, you get completely different ideas of its function. There are old-timers propping up the bar, coffee-drinking passersby, commuters in for a quick drink before the train home to suburbia, twenty-somethings on the razzle at the weekend – the Fire Station sees it all. Retaining many original features of the eponymous building, there are several spaces for drinkers or diners. Unusually the wine list doesn't seem to offer anything French (apart from Champagne), so New World devotees are well-served here. Some Spanish and Italian bottles keep it honest for those who prefer the Old World.

⊖ ⇄Waterloo (East)

Studio 6

Gabriel's Wharf, 56 Upper Ground, SE1
☎020 7928 6243
Mon-Sat: 12.30pm - 11pm
Sun: 12.30pm - 10.30pm
14 @ £2.40 - £3.95
16 @ £9.50 - £27.00

South Bank stand-by

Well situated in proximity to all the South Bank amenities, Studio 6 runs along one side of the lively Gabriel's Wharf development. There are two main spaces, both decked out in cream with bentwood bistro furniture, and a curved bar with stools for those who like a chat with the staff while ordering drinks. The wine selection comprises representatives from the main New World producers, with some Europeans for good measure. The food menu looks interesting, and with just a little stretch of the imagination, the whole package could make you think you were in California rather than beside the Thames. When the sun shines and you can use the outdoor tables, just shut your eyes and believe it.

Plus:

All Bar One

1 Chicheley Street, SE1
☎020 7921 9471

Chez Gérard at The White House

1 Belvedere Road, SE1
☎020 7202 8470

The Mulberry Bush (Young's)

89 Upper Ground, SE1
☎020 7928 7940

The Reef

Waterloo Station Concourse, SE1
☎020 7401 3686

West Hampstead

No 77

77 Mill Lane, NW6
020 7435 7787
Mon & Tue: Noon - 11pm
Wed-Sat: Noon - Midnight; Sun: 1pm - 11pm
16 @ £2.50 - £3.75 (125ml)
49 @ £9.95 - £49.95

Wine and sport do mix

Just where you least expect it, No 77 is a curious mix of serious wine bar and a collection of sports memorabilia. The décor is traditional '70s bistro-style, with quarry tiles, alcoves and potted plants, but this is secondary to the twin functions of the venue: providing a wide-ranging international choice of wines (some from mid-'90s vintages) and showcasing autographed rugby jerseys, oars, posters, and even a pair of skis from world-renowned athletes. Inevitably, big sports events are heavily promoted and customers can watch these on the bar TV, but there are other niches for those who prefer to concentrate on the wine. It's an unusual combination, but any bar which can offer Keith Wood's rugby training shirt and a decent drop of vino gets our vote.

Westminster

Westminster Arms

9 Storey's Gate, SW1
020 7222 8520
Mon-Fri: Noon - 11pm
Sat & Sun: Noon - 5pm
11 @ £2.55 - £2.90
19 @ £10.25 - £38.50

Order! Order!

The wine bar proper is known as Storey's, and is located under the pub down some metal stairs. Inside, it's traditional in every sense of the word: wooden fittings, booth seating around the edges, free-standing high tables and stools in the centre, and half-barrels hanging from the walls along with other items of wine memorabilia. Likewise, the range of wines is traditional (and very good value), with the predominantly French selection supplemented by various bottles from elsewhere. Any of these is ideal to wash down the hearty British pub grub served in the bar. In summer there is an influx of hungry tourists, but out of season this is more the haunt of local workers – and around here, that covers everything from civil servants to clerics to Members of Parliament!

Eclipse

57 High Street, Wimbledon Village, SW19
☎020 8944 7722
Mon-Wed: Noon - Midnight
Thu-Sat: Noon - 1am; Sun: Noon - 10.30pm
9 @ £3.50 - £9.00
23 @ £13.00 - £200.00

Anyone for wine?

Formerly known as Volleys, Eclipse eschews any further references to a local tennis tourney and opts instead for an upmarket image more in keeping with après-sport activity. A low-slung banquette runs around the edge of a relatively intimate room, with pouffes and low tables for good measure. Two window bays on either side of the door offer prime seating, whether with friends or enjoying one of the magazines provided for reading in a quieter moment. The wine list offers a discerning international selection, helpfully described, and there is an appealing list of cocktails, including several with a Champagne base.

Smart Alex Wine Bar

33 Wimbledon Hill Road, SW19
☎020 8947 7691
Mon-Thu: Noon - 11pm
Fri & Sat: Noon - 1am; Sun: Noon - 10.30pm
30 @ £2.50 - £5.00
36 @ £9.95 - £90.00

Cheeky choice

Situated to the rear of Young's Alexandra pub in the heart of the Wimbledon shopping area, Smart Alex offers a civilised corner in which to enjoy a glass or a bottle of wine. Although still part of the pub proper, the wine bar has its own identity, emphasised by vine stencils on pillars around the room. The bar is at the rear of a spacious drinking area, and whoever did the recent remodelling of the premises has managed to blend old and new more effectively than most. Being a Young's establishment, the wine list is reliable and covers the expected international range. Beware late weekend quaffing however; prices rise on Friday and Saturday nights.

Plus:

The Alexandra (Young's)

33 Wimbledon Hill Road, SW19
☎020 8947 7691

All Bar One

37-39 Wimbledon Hill Road, SW19
☎020 8971 9871

The Crooked Billet (Young's)

15 Crooked Billet, Wimbledon Common, SW19
☎020 8946 4942

The Dog and Fox (Young's)

24 High Street, Wimbledon Village, SW19
☎020 8946 6565

Finch's (Young's)

24 High Street, Wimbledon Village, SW19
☎020 8944 6686

The Hand in Hand (Young's)

6 Crooked Billet, Wimbledon Common, SW19
☎020 8946 5720

Pitcher & Piano

4-5 High Street, Wimbledon Village, SW19
☎020 8879 7020

The Rose and Crown (Young's)

55 High Street, Wimbledon Village, SW19
☎20 8947 4713

London is full of bar chains, from the high street to the heart of the City. You can use these brief reviews to decide if one of the chains will suit your quaffing needs. Opening hours and days vary within individual chains, depending on an outlet's location – generally, they fit in with other venues in the neighbourhood.

All Bar One

15 @ £3.80 - £5.20 (250ml)
18 @ £11.30 - £38.00

All for one and one for all

There is no doubt about it, if you see an All Bar One sign you know exactly what you are going to get inside. The only thing to distinguish one of these bars from another is the size of the space which has been fitted out with sturdy wooden furniture, blackboard menus, and a substantial bar counter with overhead billing "railway". Despite the clone-style, All Bar One is thoroughly reliable in terms of both food and drink. Wines cover the international ball park, with familiar grapes and some well-known producers (Blass and Penfolds from Australia, Montana from NZ). Unusually there are no countries listed, giving you an opportunity to test your knowledge of the wine world before ordering one of these value-for-money choices.

Balls Brothers

10 @ £3.30 - £4.50
82 @ £13.00 - £120.00

"Quality First"

Balls Brothers Wine Merchants has been dispensing wine to discerning Londoners for over 150 years, in which time it has developed a series of well-appointed and welcoming bars. Many of these are in cellars under the capital, reached down staircases lined with prints of local characters or scenes, as well as impressive-looking bottles of Champagne (alas, empty). Inside, wine memorabilia draws attention to a list which offers choices from some of the top Old and New World producers. Balls Brothers also runs regular dinners and tasting events which are publicised in-house and on its website.
www.ballsbrothers.co.uk

Chez Gérard

15 @ £2.70 - £5.20
31 @ £9.95 - £125.00

Brasserie chic

The art of steak-frites in smart surroundings is the hallmark of this French-influenced chain, in select locations throughout Central London. Each venue has its own look, but the common theme is understated elegance and comfort, whether eating or drinking. Wines focus on France, although there is representation from other world regions too. Chez Gérard offers fixed price menus as well as à la carte dining, but casual drinkers are welcome, especially in the quiet moments between lunch and dinner services.
www.santeonline.co.uk

Corney & Barrow

44 @ £2.95 - £9.90
80 @ £11.25 - £125.00

City high-flier

Of the big City wine bar chains, Corney & Barrow is probably the most forward-looking in terms of presentation and wine selection. This is not to say that wine tradition is ignored, rather that C&B has a weather-eye on the future. Venues are stylishly decorated, and manage to combine comfort and elegance. The largely corporate clientele is well-served for wining and dining, and several bars have a television on in a corner – just to keep an eye on Bloomberg of course! However, anybody with a serious interest in wine should drop in to inspect a comprehensive international selection, and sample a glass or a bottle from the informative list.
www.corney-barrow.co.uk

Davy's

16 @ £2.85 - £5.00
33 @ £11.25 - £49.95

Old faithful

The tried-and-tested formula of the cosy drinking den, with no music, sawdusted floors, dark wood, old barrels and boxes, and small-paned windows has served Davy's well over the years. More than

fifty venues across London are testament to the popularity of these comfortable wine bars, where hearty food and competitively-priced wines are available. By the same token, several of the venues have a more modern style. The majority of the wines are Davy's 'own brand', based on their experience as wine merchants since 1870, and there are frequent special offers and featured vintages. Davy's is also responsible for the Heeltap & Bumper café-bar chain which combines standard seating arrangements with more laid-back lounging areas.
www.davy.co.uk

The Fine Line

7 @ £2.70 - £3.40
29 @ £10.70 - £110.00

... with reliable wine

Fast becoming a rival to All Bar One's ubiquity, Fine Line bars are springing up all over London. The fundamental style involves pale wood, fashionable colours (currently lime, pink, purple, white and orange), and interesting lighting around the bar area. The effect is to create a series of relaxed, informal venues popular with a young crowd, but equally suitable for any age. Wines fall into the standard international selection bracket, offering no real surprises, but there is some comfort in knowing that you will get a reasonable drop in pleasant surroundings.

Jamies

38 @ £3.40 - £8.00
67 @ £13.65 - £125.00

Fizz buzz

The majority of Jamies establishments are bright and modern, often housed inside the shell of an older building. This allows the basic format to be adapted to fit the space, with comfortable seating and mellow colours designed to create a relaxed ambience. Some of the Jamies bars have retained their own characters and names, such as Betjeman's (EC1) and the Pavilion (EC2). An extensive wine list offers a good international choice, whether buying by the glass or by the bottle. Champagne is a feature, with magnums and even a Jeroboam available for purchase, so Jamies is a great place to go for a lively celebration.
www.jamiesbars.co.uk

Pitcher & Piano

10 @ £2.75 - £3.35
20 @ £11.00 - £44.00

Roll out the barrel

The Pitcher & Piano pubs fit into the standard bar chain mould, combining the domestic touch of sofas and easy chairs with more formal seating zones. For the most part, the venues are in shopping or neighbourhood areas, thus providing a welcoming location for meeting friends or putting your feet up after a bout of retail therapy. Occasionally the venue is spectacular, such as on the riverside at Richmond. The available wine comes from around the world, but concentrates on familiar grapes and styles, appealing to the quaffer in you rather than the curious connoisseur.

Young's

13 or 17@ £2.50 - £4.35
14 or 18@ £9.95 - £29.95

Brewery with a lot of bottle

Based in Wandsworth, the Young's empire spreads its tentacles across London and around the UK. Young's venues come in different guises, from pubs with excellent wine selections, to specialist bars which offer a wider range. It is still unusual for a UK brewing concern to put an emphasis on its wine list, so the company has stolen a march on much of the competition. Where you see a Young's sign, you can be sure that the available wine will have been thoughtfully chosen and well-looked after. The number of wines available depends on the venue. Popping in to the pub for a swift one takes on new meaning when the choice extends beyond a pint (delicious though that can be!). Young's also promotes wine education through tasting courses arranged in some of its venues.
www.youngs.co.uk

Specialists

Many quaffing venues around London offer a broad selection of wines from all over the world. However, there are some venues which specialise in wines from specific areas. Visit any of these, and you will have an excellent opportunity to familiarise youself with the best these regions can offer.

Australasia

Cork & Bottle
Hanover Square Wine Bar
The Providores
Suze
Suze in Mayfair

Champagne

Fishmarket
La Grande Marque
Kettner's
Vertigo
Wine Wharf

France

L'Artiste Musclé
Le Bar des Amis
Le Bar du Marché
Le Beaujolais
Garrick
Cellar Gascon
The French House
Mustard's Smithfield Brasserie
Nicolas Bar à Vins
Odette's
La Tartine

Italy

Annabella Wine Bar & Restaurant
Azzurro
The Bull and Last
Isola
Osteria Pulcinella
Our Cellar
Signor Zilli
Vino

Organic

The Duke of Cambridge

Portugal

Bar Estrela

Spain

Barcelona
Goya
Leadenhall Wine & Tapas Bar
Meson Don Felipe
El Parador

Quaffers London
Wine Walks

Barbican to Tate Modern

This route will take you from one side of historical London to the other via the City; the direction you choose will be dictated by whether you prefer to end up in a world-renowned art gallery or in a top-notch arts centre.

Because so much of this route takes in the financial district, it is advisable to follow it on a weekday. Despite the area being chock-a-block with drinking and dining opportunities, it becomes a ghost town at weekends and no amount of money will change that.

Barbican Tube is on the Circle, Metropolitan, and Hammersmith & City lines. There are rail connections at nearby Farringdon and Moorgate.

Barbican Tube
Cloth Fair
London Wall
City of London
Liverpool Street Station
Tower 42
Stock Exchange
Bank of England
St Paul's Cathedral
Millennium Bridge
Tate Modern

- Starting at the Barbican Tube, you could abandon the route immediately and head north into the historically-charged area of Clerkenwell. There are monuments and remnants of centuries-old buildings tucked in among more modern architecture, which itself is being redeveloped from offices and warehouses into housing and a thriving arts and entertainment community. Look out for the many signboards indicating walking routes through the area.
- Likewise you could choose to explore the Barbican Centre, London home of the Royal Shakespeare Company, as well as cinemas, an orchestra, exhibition rooms, and several cafés and restaurants.
- However this will not get you to the other side of the Thames! From the Barbican Tube, look out for signs towards Cloth Fair, squeezed in parallel to Long Lane. This quiet cobbled street might make you feel as if you had been transported to another age. The church is opposite painted, restored houses jammed up together, one of which has been transformed into a Jamies bar: Betjeman's.
- At the far end of Cloth Fair you will come out opposite the Smithfield market. If the stalls are open, wander around to catch some of the capital's finest traders in action. Don't forget to look up – the buildings' ornamentation deserves notice. At other times of day it is less lively, so Cellar Gascon on West Smithfield Circle is an ideal spot for a quick glass of something from South-Western France. (A visit to their delicatessen, Comptoir Gascon, in Charterhouse Street, on the far side of the market, is worth a detour if you are after fine products from the French gourmet heartland.)
- On the south side of the circle you have the William Wallace memorial, a must-see for Scots everywhere, on the wall of St Bartholomew's hospital. To the left of the memorial, go down Little Britain to the junction with Montague Street. Turn left towards a major roundabout, and cross over to London Wall. This is the ancient bounds of the City of London, chunks of which stud the modern City. The Museum of London is signposted, as are the Highwalks which link the office buildings above street-level. For an imposing impression of concrete canyons you can't beat it.
- El Vino on the Bastion Highwalk right near the Museum can provide refreshment before you continue along London Wall past Moorgate Tube.

- At Old Broad Street you could detour left to Liverpool Street station and beyond that to the Broadgate complex, an office and leisure architectural package which even has a winter ice rink. However, going right at this junction keeps you on the route.
- This being the City, the wine bars of Davy's, Corney & Barrow and Balls Brothers are everywhere you turn, along with plenty of interesting alternatives. One of the most spectacular, but which requires planning ahead, is Twenty-Four in Tower 42 on Old Broad Street. From here you get fantastic views over the capital, but this privilege needs to be booked in advance to avoid disappointment. Those with a real head for heights could try Vertigo on the top floor of the same building.
- Carry on down Old Broad Street past the Stock Exchange to the Royal Exchange Buildings, as featured at the end of the recent film "Bridget Jones' Diary". There is a tiny Corney & Barrow here, with outdoor tables in the plaza for sampling London's better weather if it's summertime. You will reach the traditional nerve-centre of Britain's financial policy at Bank, but the closest you'll get to experiencing the cut-and-thrust will be at the Museum of the Bank of England.
- Shopping opportunities present themselves as you stroll along Poultry and then Cheapside, heading for St Paul's Cathedral. A diversion right into Wood Street will lead you to the Monk Exchange, a good place for a snack, a comfortable chair, and a glass of thirst-quenching quaffing wine.
- St Paul's dominates the landscape and all roads here seem to lead to it. As you approach the back of the cathedral from Cheapside, look out for a Balls Brothers wine bar on your left. Again there is outdoor seating available in a small piazza under the watchful eye of a gilded statue of the saint, standing in St Paul's Churchyard across the road.
- No visit to London would be complete without investigating Christopher Wren's landmark cathedral further, either by circumnavigating the exterior or by going in for the full tour.
- However, London's latest international icon awaits on the south bank of the Thames: the Tate Modern gallery, characterised by the enormous single chimney left over from its days as a power station. Your link between these two symbols of London is the brand-new Millennium Bridge, reached by walking across the broad promenade of Peter's Hill on the river side of St Paul's.
- Should the bridge still be closed to pedestrians… from St Paul's, walk down to Blackfriars Bridge, either by following the main road via Ludgate Hill and Ludgate Circus then turn left to the river, or meander through the local alleys and by-ways for a less orthodox experience.
- Once across the Thames, you will be in Southwark, and could end here with a well-earned break in the Tate Café, or join Wine Route I along Bankside to the East or the West.

London Bridge to Waterloo

The south side of the River Thames is home to a huge variety of places of interest for Londoners and visitors alike. From the historic haunts of The Borough, along Bankside towards the theatres and concert halls of the South Bank at Waterloo, there really is something for everyone.

This route starts the same but then splits to offer two ways of reaching Waterloo. Neither is far apart so any amount of zig-zagging can allow you to get the best of both if you are so inclined. Have the street map handy just in case!

London Bridge Station is on the Jubilee and Northern (branch) Tube lines, and also has rail connections to the South-East.

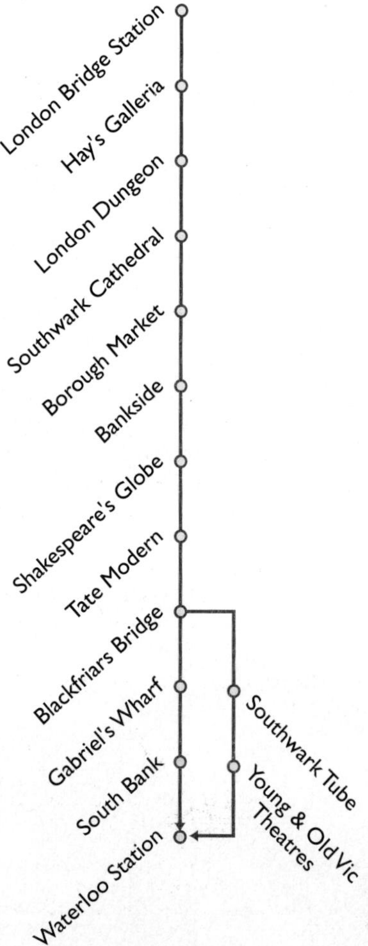

- There is an excellent view of Tower Bridge from the riverside at Hay's Galleria in Tooley Street, beside HMS Belfast. Follow this with a glass in Balls Brothers in the Galleria, or in any of three Davy's wine bars (the Cooperage, Skinkers or the Mughouse) in Tooley Street. Each has a different atmosphere but the same comprehensive Davy's wine list and hearty food.
- Queue for the London Dungeon in Tooley Street, or visit the lesser-known Old Operating Theatre Museum & Herb Garret in St Thomas Street, near the hospital on the other side of London Bridge Station.
- Cross over Borough High Street just by the bridge, and go down some steps next to Southwark Cathedral to enter Borough Market. The market, under the railway arches, is a great place to find gourmet treats and ingredients, fruit and vegetables. There is record of a market on this site since the 11th century.
- On the far side of the market, look for Wine Wharf which has over 200 wines by the glass or bottle. Alternatively, go through Majestic Wines into the Vinopolis shop: books, gadgets, glasses, and some seriously fine wines for the dedicated quaffer. You can also join a Vinopolis tour, which should be booked in advance.
- Continue through the shop to Cantina Vinopolis for more wine or some food, or consider back-tracking slightly around the market and Southwark Cathedral to the river so you can see the replica of the ship "Golden Hinde".
- Stroll along Clink Street past historic excavations and the Prison Museum, a dark and forboding reminder of the past which is signalled by some gruesome-looking skeletons. And yes, this street is why some people still call prison 'the clink'.
- Stay with the signposted Bankside river walk (under Southwark Bridge, past the Rose Theatre) until you reach Shakespeare's Globe. The lodgings allegedly occupied by Sir Christopher Wren while he oversaw the construction of St Paul's Cathedral in the late 17th century are next door – a tiny pink house on the riverside.

- From here it's no distance past the Millennium Bridge to Tate Modern, as much of a landmark south of the river as St Paul's Cathedral is on the other side. The Tate Café has a reasonable wine selection but is often very busy.
- The route splits at Blackfriars Bridge. The first stays with the river, the second drops back into Southwark.

The river route

- From Blackfriars Bridge onward you will notice second-hand booksellers in all sorts of places – under arches, out in the open, in subways or underpasses. It's worth rummaging for bargains.
- At Gabriel's Wharf there are speciality shops and a lively atmosphere which children will enjoy. At the back of this area is a Young's pub, The Mulberry Bush, with a good choice of wines, or you could enjoy a glass at Studio 6 within the wharf area.
- By now the mid-20th century architecture of the South Bank will be looming before you. Choose from the National Theatre, the Royal Festival Hall, the Museum of the Moving Image (MOMI), the National Film Theatre and the Hayward Gallery. For the first two it is advisable to have booked tickets in advance for performances, unless you want to queue for returns.
- From the Festival Hall, promenade along Concert Hall Approach and stop in at the Archduke. Musicians often come here between rehearsals and concerts, and live jazz in the evenings is a feature. Waterloo Station is opposite the end of the Approach.

The Southwark route

- At Blackfriars Bridge, go up steps to street level and walk due south down Blackfriars Road (away from the river). Look for Scoresby Street on your left just before the overhead railway bridge. Down here you will find Blackfriars Wine Bar, in the traditional mould, run and enjoyed by locals.
- At Southwark Underground Station go right along The Cut. There are plenty of bars and restaurants for all tastes here. Meson Don Felipe specialises in authentic Spanish wines and tapas. Bar Citrus offers a reasonable range of wines as well as other beverages, and food. The Young Vic and Old Vic theatres can both be found on this stretch of road.
- As you near the end of The Cut you are approaching Waterloo Station. Cross the road to the Fire Station which is a bustling food, drink and social venue at most times of the day.

At Waterloo

- The famous station, under whose four-sided clock many a tryst has been made, contains the Eurostar terminal, and you can catch trains to most points south too. The Tube is on the Jubilee, Bakerloo and Northern (branch) lines.
- The London IMAX Cinema is in the centre of the big roundabout outside the station. West of the station along York Road are the "London Eye" Millennium Wheel (advance booking essential), London Aquarium and former County Hall.

To regain the north side of the river without going below ground, use Westminster Bridge by County Hall (to the Houses of Parliament and Westminster Tube), or Hungerford Foot Bridge by the Royal Festival Hall (to Embankment Tube).

St Paul's to Trafalgar Square

Some parts of London are so packed with things to see and do that it can be difficult to choose, particularly if time is of the essence. Likewise it can be hard to create a practical route if you are new to London's idiosyncratic patchwork of streets, alleys and lanes.

This route wends its way through some of the capital's best-known tourist spots, hopefully avoiding too many traps, and also providing inspiration for city-dwelling wine drinkers to explore familiar territory further.

St Paul's is on the Central underground line. Mansion House and Blackfriars Stations, on both the Circle and District lines, are also nearby, and may be more convenient. This route involves some serious legwork – use the No.11 London Bus to get you from A to B more quickly. It runs from St Paul's along Fleet Street and the Strand to Trafalgar Square, then continues to Parliament and Westminster Abbey. If you have a Travelcard you can hop on and off at will. The conductors are extremely helpful and will tell you when to alight for different destinations.

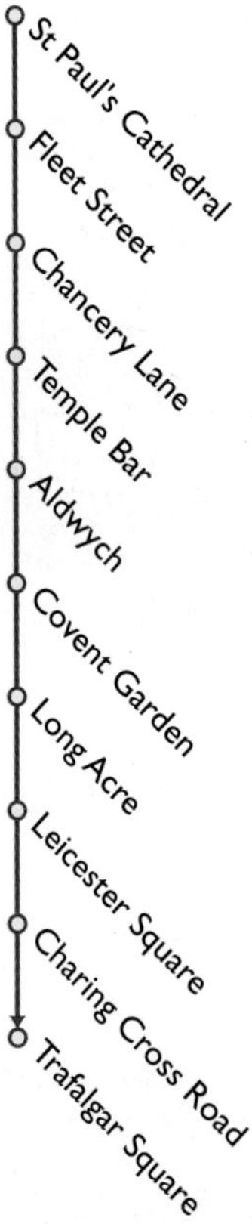

St Paul's Cathedral
Fleet Street
Chancery Lane
Temple Bar
Aldwych
Covent Garden
Long Acre
Leicester Square
Charing Cross Road
Trafalgar Square

- From the steps of St Paul's Cathedral, walk down Ludgate Hill to Ludgate Circus. Straight across the junction is Fleet Street, former home to the London press corps. The Reuters building on the left-hand side and the Daily Express on the right (with a spectacular gilt and chrome foyer – London's answer to New York's Chrysler Buiding, at least on the inside!) still have premises here.
- The Wine Press (right side) has decent wines and delicious Italian food at reasonable prices. El Vino (left side) has a great selection and also does off-licence sales. Everywhere in the area gets packed with City workers, but you don't need to be wearing a suit to enjoy the atmosphere.
- Just before Temple Bar at the end of Fleet Street you could divert right, up Chancery Lane. Here on the right (quite a long way up) are the London Silver Vaults, a fascinating collection of silversmiths and merchants. If it's made in silver you can find it here without breaking the bank – one of London's best-kept secrets.
- In Chancery Lane enjoy the classy sophistication of Hodgson's, or make for Cort's – the original independent wine bar in this part of town. Both are below street level on the left side of the lane.
- At Temple Bar the neo-Gothic façade of the Royal Courts of Justice marks the start of the Strand. Tucked in to the corner opposite the courts is Daly's, likely to be busy with lawyers and their clients.
- Aldwych, with Bush House (home of the BBC World Service), is on the right of the Strand. Bank or the Columbia offer a wide selection of drinks. On the left, beside King's College London, is the recently refurbished Somerset House and the Courtauld Institute. Nearby is Covent Garden with its Piazza and Marketplace: The London Transport Museum and the Royal Opera House are just two of the attractions here.
- Covent Garden is full of places to eat and drink, with varying quality and price. Check any menus you see outside an establishment before going in, although nobody should mind if you get inside and then change your mind before being seated.
- To escape from the scrum of tourists and street artists vying for your attention, go upstairs in the South Market to Chez Gérard Opera Terrace. From the bar you can overlook the Opera House but still feel part of the action. Hidden away behind the Opera House in Hanover Place is the Bar des Amis du Vin. They serve a wonderful choice of cheeses from chunks kept behind the bar, not to mention excellent wines.

- Music-lovers should go into the well of the covered market (southside) to the Crusting Pipe, a Davy's wine bar in every respect – but with impromptu performances from local musicians. This is a great refuge, especially if it's raining but you still want entertainment and relatively fresh air.
- Tear yourself away from the Garden's delights, and head in the direction of the Tube station to Long Acre. There are plenty of quality chain stores here, as well as some speciality boutiques, making it a good alternative to some of London's busier shopping zones.
- Go left down Long Acre towards Leicester Square. At the junction with Charing Cross Road, pause... the next move is crucial, depending on how much you would like a top-notch glass of wine; there are two possibilities.

Detour into Leicester Square (almost!)

- Continue towards the tourist Mecca that is the square – ticket agencies, cinemas, touts, and more people clutching a street map and speaking different languages than you ever thought existed. By the same token, the number of people ready to rip you off one way or another also increases. This is the place to be more vigilant than ever.
- Give yourself a break by descending into the Cork & Bottle, cunningly disguised on the left just before you hit the square proper. Your patience in locating it will be rewarded, and there is a good chance that this will be the end of your wine walk through London for the day – it takes that long to read the fantastic list before choosing! When you eventually emerge, retrace your steps to Charing Cross Road.

- Detour or not, the last stages of the route are the same. Go down Charing Cross Road (left from Long Acre or right from Leicester Square). The National Portrait Gallery on the right is an excellent free museum and has a fantastic and unusual view from its bar-restaurant, the Portrait, on the top floor.
- Corney & Barrow, opposite the Portrait Gallery, offers an impressive range of wines by the glass or the bottle, as well as food. Don't be put off by its austere ex-bank exterior and its modern minimalist interior. You're there for the wine.
- The parish church of St Martin in the Fields on the left introduces you to Trafalgar Square, with Nelson's Column, the National Gallery, and any number of embassies nearby. St Martin's holds regular services and concerts (lunchtimes and evenings – check notices outside); its musicians have an international reputation.
- From Nelson you will be able to see the expanse of Whitehall towards Horseguards Parade, the Cenotaph and Parliament Square, as well as Buckingham Palace in the distance through Admiralty Arch. Don't forget to see what currently occupies the fourth plinth in Trafalgar Square's north-west corner – London's most hotly-debated piece of real estate, after it was left empty when the square was originally constructed.
- Beside the church, walk along Duncannon Street to the Strand. Cross over to Villiers Street, with Charing Cross Station immediately on your right. As the street flattens out, look left for an unpromising door with signs for Gordon's. Descend the narrow stairs to a long-standing haven of wine-drinking pleasure, with food to match – the ideal venue in which to finish a stimulating day.

Think of London, and images of Parliament, royalty, famous churches and bastions of culture are never far from mind. This walk combines all of these faces of the capital, with a couple of London's beautiful parks included for good measure.

- Victoria Station
- Westminster Cathedral
- Parliament Square
- Westminster Abbey
- Houses of Parliament
- St James's Park
- Buckingham Palace
- Green Park
- Piccadilly Circus
- Regent Street
- Oxford Circus
- Soho
- Chinatown
- Tottenham Court Road
- British Museum

There are so many possibilities for getting from start to finish of this route that it's worth consulting your street guide for interesting diversions off the basic trail, other than those which are suggested here. Depending on your focus you can concentrate on history or contemporary culture, but the parks are not to be missed – tranquil havens in the heart of the city.

Victoria station is on the Circle, District and Victoria lines, and is a major transport hub in the capital.

- At Victoria Station grab a quick refreshment in the concourse café the Reef, or outside the station, cross the road to Justin de Blank where you can watch the crowds from inside, but they can't see you.
- Not far along Victoria Street lies the neo-Byzantine Catholic Westminster Cathedral, not to be confused with its Anglican counterpart further down the same road. Set back from the road in an impressive piazza, it provides a marked contrast to some of London's other well-known religious architecture. Either continue along Victoria Street to Parliament Square, or take a slight detour into Buckingham Gate, where ultra-modern Zander livens up the local civil service buildings. Go along Petty France past St James's Tube station to Tothill Street which also leads into Parliament Square.
- It would take more than a day to do justice to the sites of interest around this one small part of London. While you are deciding whether to tackle Westminster Abbey, Methodist Central Hall, the Houses of Parliament, or simply gaze on the river from Westminster Bridge as William Wordsworth once did, call into the Westminster Arms in Storey's Gate where the cellar bar offers a decent selection of quaffing wines.
- Whitehall, the Cenotaph, a peek at Downing Street, and the mounted soldiers outside Horseguards Parade may draw you along the tarmac trail towards Trafalgar Square, but with the lush oasis of St James's Park so near, why not take the green route? Reach it from Parliament Square by walking along Great George Street. Once in the park there are plenty of possibilities: head west for the Victoria Memorial opposite Buckingham Palace (although you can catch glimpses of both as you stroll), or aim for St James's Palace and Clarence House, where Prince Charles and the Queen Mother have their London homes.
- Step outside the park for refreshment in St James's Street, perhaps at Just Oriental, Davy's at St James's or Balls Brothers. If you are in the market to purchase fine wines, many of the UK's top merchants have their headquarters in historical buildings on this thoroughfare.
- Make your way into Green Park and head up the gently sloping ground to Piccadilly. You may wish to duck into Mayfair to visit L'Artiste Musclé in Shepherd Market, or seek out the designer shops on New Bond Street. Just before Piccadilly Circus, look for the Waterstone's bookshop on the right. From the fifth floor Studio Lounge there's a great view, with the added bonus of wandering through Europe's biggest bookstore.

- From Piccadilly Circus, with its neon signs and statue of Eros, make for the elegant sweep of Regent Street. L'Odéon affords a peaceful view of the bustle, from its upstairs location under the arches. Famous London toystore Hamleys is on the right, and here you can buy a copy of the Quaffers® game.
- Running parallel to Regent Street, Kingly Street is home to top quaff spot Shampers, and there is access to the contrasting fashion and style of Carnaby Street and Liberty of London. If you survive the shopping opportunities of Regent Street, further temptation awaits in Oxford Street. Go right at Oxford Circus, brave the crowds, and strike out for the junction with Tottenham Court Road.
- Alternatively, you may choose to meander through Soho, where every second place is a bar or restaurant. Kettner's is fantastic for Champagne, but there is an endless choice of venues. Le Bar du Marché in Berwick Market is another excellent option, in among the fruit and flower sellers and fabric shops which fill this pedestrianised zone.
- If time is short, skirt the edges of Soho along Shaftesbury Avenue, past Chinatown on the right, to Cambridge Circus. Nearby, Le Beaujolais in Litchfield Street is a shrine to Gamay grapes. The bookshops on Charing Cross Road en route to Tottenham Court Road are likely to delay you, with the organised chaos of Foyle's the most celebrated of the many examples which line the road. Don't miss number 84!
- A relaxed quaff at the Grape Street Wine Bar will prepare you for the last leg of the route, along Bloomsbury Street to Bedford Square. If you haven't already succumbed to an overwhelming amount of culture, there is always the British Museum with its vast collections, and the new Reading Room in its Great Court. On the far side of the museum, Russell Square Tube beckons to take you home.

Tube and rail stations

Venues

E

F

G

H

I

J

QUAFFERS

Open at weekends

Open at weekends

Quaff some wine • Run a vineyard • Laugh a lot • Learn something

"What I really like about Quaffers is that it combines amusement and education with the chance to have a few bevvies."
Tim Atkin, The Observer.

It's about having fun while learning about wine! The board game is for 4 or more adults and key features include blind tasting and the testing of wine knowledge through answering 'Experience' questions of varying levels of difficulty.

To find out more about the game, visit www.quaffers.co.uk/game
Order online, or simply use the order form overleaf!

Quaffers™ **HOW TO ORDER YOUR COPY**

by post

Please use BLOCK CAPITALS!

Quaffers® Wine Game Order
ChonkyChonks Ltd
60, East St Helen Street
Abingdon
Oxon OX14 5EB

by telephone

Call **01235 535685** for sales and enquiries

by fax or internet

Fill in this order form and FAX it to **01235 537312**

or visit the shop page at the Quaffers® website:
http://**www.quaffers.co.uk**

Customer's Name ....

Delivery Address ....

....

Postcode ....

Daytime Telephone .... **E-mail** ....

	Quantity	Unit Price	Cost(£)
Quaffers® Wine Game		£35.99	
Subtotal			
post and packing		£3.50	
Total Amount Payable			

Method of Payment

Cheques should be made out to: **ChonkyChonks Ltd.** Please tick the correct payment box.

By Cheque: ☐ By Credit Card: ☐ Visa ☐ MasterCard ☐ Switch/Delta

Card Number: ☐☐☐☐ ☐☐☐☐ ☐☐☐☐ ☐☐☐☐ Card Expiry Date: ☐☐ ☐☐ Switch Issue Number ☐☐

Name (as it appears on the card) ....

Date .... **Signature** ....

Want to have fun and learn about wine?

I know millions of you do. That is why, in 1999, I started ChonkyChonks – a company devoted to providing fun education and information about wine.

It's so easy to be overwhelmed by the choice of wines now available, frustrated by the lack of guidance or information when we want to buy, and put off by the expense or formality often associated with wine education that is on offer.

At ChonkyChonks we offer a solution. We have created exciting products and services, under the Quaffers® brand, that give plenty of useful information about wine in a relaxed and informal way. Why not find out more, and take greater delight in your quaffing?

We have jam-packed our website **www.quaffers.co.uk** with all sorts of fun entertainment about wine. There are monthly features, weekly wine tastings and bar reviews, competitions, quizzes, interesting facts, and many opportunities for our community of wine-lovers to have their say and tell us about what they like (and dislike) about wine. Of course, we also tell you lots about the Quaffers® products and services and provide a secure shop so that you can buy our products while online. Why not take a look and join in the fun too?

Quaffers® branded products and services include:

Products:

Quaffers® Wine Board Game – own a vineyard, taste wines blind and answer questions about wine!
Quaffers® Experience Cards
Quaffers® Trumps (coming soon!)
Quaffers® London: Where to quaff wine in the capital

Services:

Quaffers® Tasting Events
Quaffers® Corporate Blind Wine Tasting and Quiz Championship

Have fun learning more about wine, and happy quaffing!

Heather

Heather Miller
heather@chonkychonks.co.uk

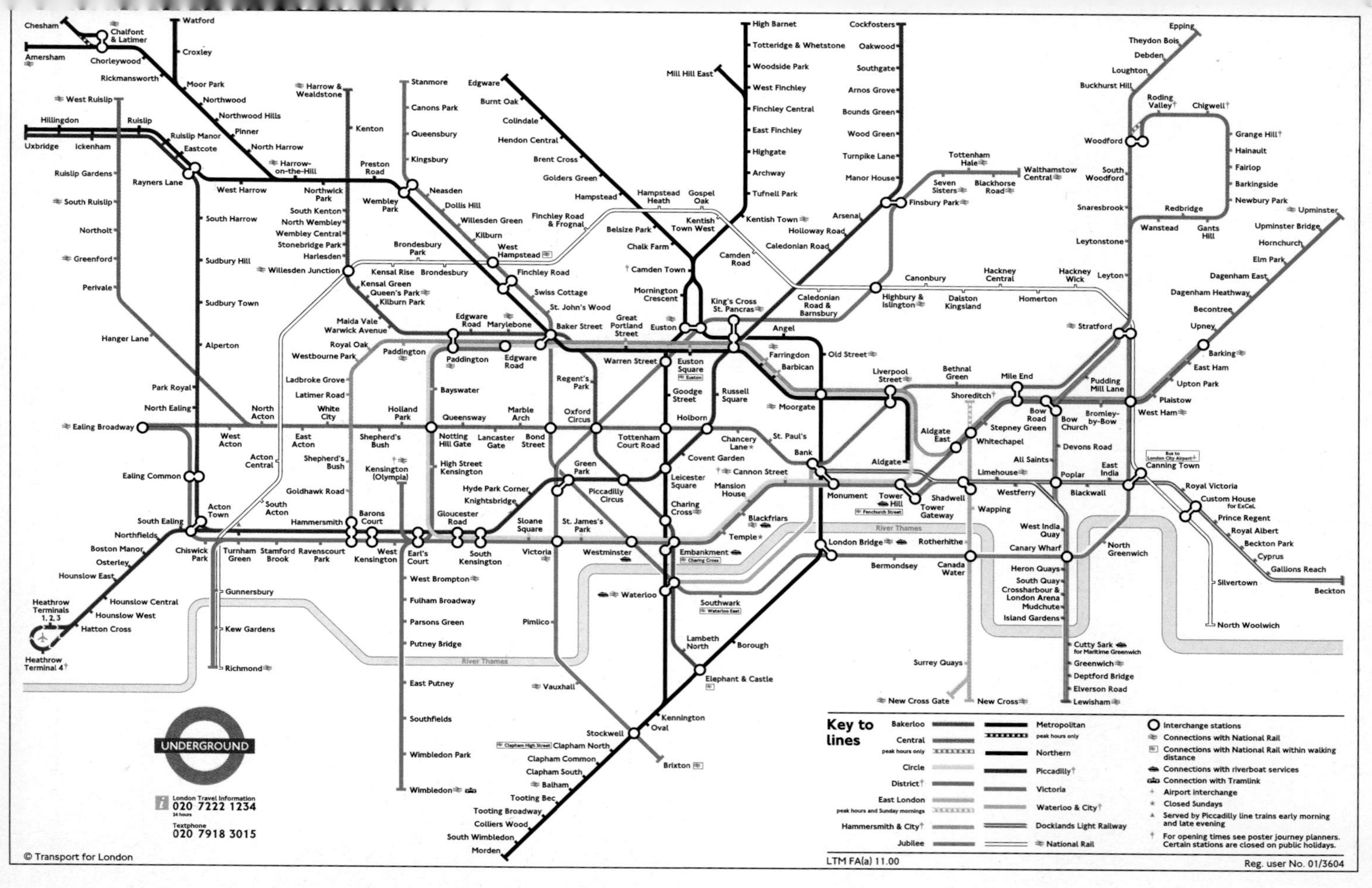
Chesham
Chalfont & Latimer
Amersham
Chorleywood
Rickmansworth
Watford
Croxley
Moor Park
Northwood
Northwood Hills
Pinner
North Harrow
Harrow-on-the-Hill
West Ruislip
Hillingdon
Ruislip
Ruislip Manor
Eastcote
Uxbridge
Ickenham
Ruislip Gardens
South Ruislip
Rayners Lane
West Harrow
South Harrow
Northolt
Greenford
Perivale
Sudbury Hill
Sudbury Town
Alperton
Hanger Lane
Park Royal
North Ealing
Ealing Broadway
West Acton
North Acton
East Acton
Acton Central
Ealing Common
South Ealing
Acton Town
South Acton
Northfields
Boston Manor
Osterley
Hounslow East
Hounslow Central
Hounslow West
Hatton Cross
Heathrow Terminals 1, 2, 3
Heathrow Terminal 4
Chiswick Park
Turnham Green
Stamford Brook
Ravenscourt Park
Gunnersbury
Kew Gardens
Richmond
Harrow & Wealdstone
Kenton
Preston Road
Northwick Park
South Kenton
North Wembley
Wembley Central
Stonebridge Park
Harlesden
Willesden Junction
Wembley Park
Stanmore
Canons Park
Queensbury
Kingsbury
Neasden
Dollis Hill
Willesden Green
Kilburn
Brondesbury Park
Kensal Rise
Brondesbury
Kensal Green
Queen's Park
Kilburn Park
Maida Vale
Warwick Avenue
Royal Oak
Westbourne Park
Ladbroke Grove
Latimer Road
White City
Shepherd's Bush
Goldhawk Road
Hammersmith
Barons Court
West Kensington
Kensington (Olympia)
Holland Park
Edgware
Burnt Oak
Colindale
Hendon Central
Brent Cross
Golders Green
Hampstead
Finchley Road & Frognal
West Hampstead
Finchley Road
Swiss Cottage
St. John's Wood
Belsize Park
Chalk Farm
Hampstead Heath
Gospel Oak
Kentish Town West
Camden Town
Camden Road
Mill Hill East
High Barnet
Totteridge & Whetstone
Woodside Park
West Finchley
Finchley Central
East Finchley
Highgate
Archway
Tufnell Park
Kentish Town
Cockfosters
Oakwood
Southgate
Arnos Grove
Bounds Green
Wood Green
Turnpike Lane
Manor House
Arsenal
Holloway Road
Caledonian Road
Finsbury Park
Seven Sisters
Tottenham Hale
Blackhorse Road
Walthamstow Central
Mornington Crescent
King's Cross St. Pancras
Caledonian Road & Barnsbury
Highbury & Islington
Canonbury
Dalston Kingsland
Hackney Central
Homerton
Hackney Wick
Leyton
Edgware Road
Marylebone
Baker Street
Great Portland Street
Euston
Paddington
Edgware Road
Bayswater
Notting Hill Gate
Queensway
Lancaster Gate
Marble Arch
Bond Street
Regent's Park
Oxford Circus
Warren Street
Euston Square
Goodge Street
Tottenham Court Road
Russell Square
Holborn
Angel
Farringdon
Barbican
Old Street
Moorgate
Liverpool Street
Bethnal Green
Mile End
High Street Kensington
Hyde Park Corner
Knightsbridge
Green Park
Piccadilly Circus
Leicester Square
Covent Garden
Chancery Lane
St. Paul's
Bank
Cannon Street
Mansion House
Charing Cross
Gloucester Road
South Kensington
Sloane Square
St. James's Park
Victoria
Westminster
Embankment
Temple
Blackfriars
Monument
Tower Hill
Fenchurch Street
Tower Gateway
Aldgate
Aldgate East
Shoreditch
Whitechapel
Stepney Green
Shadwell
Wapping
Earl's Court
West Brompton
Fulham Broadway
Parsons Green
Putney Bridge
East Putney
Southfields
Wimbledon Park
Wimbledon
Pimlico
Vauxhall
Waterloo
Southwark
Waterloo East
Lambeth North
Elephant & Castle
Borough
London Bridge
Bermondsey
Rotherhithe
Canada Water
Surrey Quays
New Cross Gate
New Cross
Stockwell
Kennington
Oval
Brixton
Clapham North
Clapham High Street
Clapham Common
Clapham South
Balham
Tooting Bec
Tooting Broadway
Colliers Wood
South Wimbledon
Morden
River Thames
Stratford
Pudding Mill Lane
Bow Road
Bow Church
Bromley-by-Bow
West Ham
Devons Road
All Saints
Limehouse
Westferry
Poplar
East India
Blackwall
West India Quay
Canary Wharf
Heron Quays
South Quay
Crossharbour & London Arena
Mudchute
Island Gardens
Cutty Sark for Maritime Greenwich
Greenwich
Deptford Bridge
Elverson Road
Lewisham
North Greenwich
Canning Town
Bus to London City Airport
Royal Victoria
Custom House for ExCeL
Prince Regent
Royal Albert
Beckton Park
Cyprus
Gallions Reach
Beckton
Silvertown
North Woolwich
Plaistow
Upton Park
East Ham
Barking
Upney
Becontree
Dagenham Heathway
Dagenham East
Elm Park
Hornchurch
Upminster Bridge
Upminster
Epping
Theydon Bois
Debden
Loughton
Buckhurst Hill
Roding Valley
Chigwell
Grange Hill
Hainault
Fairlop
Barkingside
Newbury Park
Woodford
South Woodford
Snaresbrook
Redbridge
Leytonstone
Wanstead
Gants Hill
UNDERGROUND
London Travel Information
020 7222 1234
24 hours
Textphone
020 7918 3015
© Transport for London
Key to lines
Bakerloo
Central
peak hours only
Circle
District
East London
peak hours and Sunday mornings
Hammersmith & City
Jubilee
Metropolitan
peak hours only
Northern
Piccadilly
Victoria
Waterloo & City
Docklands Light Railway
National Rail
Interchange stations
Connections with National Rail
Connections with National Rail within walking distance
Connections with riverboat services
Connection with Tramlink
Airport interchange
Closed Sundays
Served by Piccadilly line trains early morning and late evening
For opening times see poster journey planners. Certain stations are closed on public holidays.
LTM FA(a) 11.00
Reg. user No. 01/3604